SALAD DAYS

A NOVEL BY

FRANCES BADALAMENTI

Salad Days

Published by Unsolicited Press
Printed in the United States of America.
First Edition:

For information contact:
Unsolicited Press
Portland, Oregon
www.unsolicitedpress.com
orders@unsolicitedpress.com

Cover design: John Phemister
Editor: S.R. Stewart

ISBN: 978-1-950730-39-1

SALAD DAYS

A NOVEL BY

FRANCES BADALAMENTI

For John

You are here with me
You have been here, and you are everything

—R.E.M.

One

Portland

I leaned my ratty, forest green three-speed bike on the porch and let myself into a small, not very well-kept bungalow off Northeast Alberta Street. I headed into the kitchen, passing a pile of dirty dishes, coffee dregs in a pot, and a glass ashtray with a half-smoked cigarette stubbed out and perched in a groove. I grabbed the cigarette out of the ashtray and followed a trail of wet footprints through the hallway. Loud music radiated through the drafty old house. Between the piercing music, the lingering smell of fried garlic and Nag Champa incense, and the events of the past few weeks, I had to lean onto the counter because I felt dizzy.

"Anyone fucking here?" I asked. "Is anybody home?" I yelled.

I headed toward the back of the house, hovering in the hallway. I took a few more steps and could hear running water coming from the bath. The old floorboards creaked. I peeked inside the bathroom and found Jess alone in the tub with a dark green clay mask encrusting her face. All I saw were these wide, dark eyes staring back at me. The water ran fast and hard. Archers of Loaf's album *Icky Mettle* was on super high volume, preventing any chance of verbal exchange between me and this person who I had met only a few months ago, who came from where I came from, and who had become a crucial, codependent part of my new life in a new city.

I sat on the toilet and lit the half-smoked cigarette with a lighter that I found on the windowsill. I took a drag and handed the cigarette over to Jess. We looked at each other. She took a drag and passed the cigarette back to me. I smoked and gazed out the window into the overgrown backyard, past the blackberry brambles, the huge weeds, and the tall, uncut grass, and a detached garage with a moss-covered roof.

A few months ago, my husband Paul and I attended a group art show that Jess had put together in that garage. It was soon after we had uprooted from Jersey and replanted ourselves in the Pacific Northwest. The combination of that unfamiliar environment and the scents of cedar fencing, wet dirt, and dense weed made me feel alive in a way that I had never felt before.

Everything was still so novel back then: the smells, the visuals, and the people. It was still like a dream; it was like living in a dream.

That evening, as I wandered around, pretending to be interested in the artwork, Paul stood in a corner, gripping a can of cheap beer and chatting with people we didn't yet know. There were about ten shoddy paintings, a few framed pencil drawings, and a bunch of black and white photo prints nailed or tacked to the dusty garage rafters. I had never been to a backyard art show before, just the stark white galleries of

Manhattan where one often feels scrutinized, uneducated, and lesser.

I felt at ease and curious in Jess's garage, even though the work was so amateur. I was more interested in the people anyhow. We were all somewhere in our twenties, had transplanted ourselves to Portland, and had creative aspirations of some kind. We all wanted to live somewhere that had affordable housing, maybe even a small patch of grass where I could grow food and pot.

There was no talk of the stresses of living in Manhattan or Brooklyn, nothing about the rising costs of rent, and no utterings about the existential boredom of mundane cubical life. Most people who Jess knew worked in coffee shops and restaurants and bars. And that is exactly why Paul and I left when we did. We didn't want the pressure to live a certain kind of life, the pining of a certain type of career, just in order to make ends meet. At first, we thought it would be San Francisco or Seattle, but those cities had gotten too intense and too expensive, so it ended up being Portland.

It was that night in the moldy garage that made us feel like we had truly arrived, as if we had taken the best parts of what we left back in Milltown and transported them out to Oregon.

Jess leaned back and closed her eyes. I remained on the toilet with my head in my hands. Dana came out of her bedroom, wearing a black string bikini, her face also covered in splotchy green, drying clay. She closed the bathroom door and slithered into the tub. The bubbly water almost overflowed onto the floor. Jess turned off the running water, and the small room finally quieted to a gentle hum.

All that could be heard was the droning sounds of the music blasting from the living room and the splashes from the tub.

I remembered the night when Archers of Loaf played at Milltown Tavern, the indie music venue in Milltown where Dana and I had met and where we had worked together. I thought about how packed the band room was that night, how you could hardly move through the crowd, and how I was alone working behind the small back bar, other than a few visits from Mark to change kegs, to restock cups, and to dump big plastic buckets of ice into the metal cooler. The crowd seemed so much older and way more mature than I was, like they were so much smarter, way more refined. They seemed so much better than me.

"What's up with the bathing suit?" I asked Dana.

"She didn't want you seeing her boobs!" Jess said, laughing.

Then Dana laughed so hard that chunks of the mask cracked off her face, huge green flakes falling into the tub.

"Jesus! Look what you're doing, Dana!" Jess snapped.

"Oh, shut the fuck up!" Dana barked back.

"You're gonna leave Paul for that guy, aren't you?" Dana asked, palming a ball of bath bubbles and blowing them into the tub.

"Wait, have you done anything with him yet?" Jess interjected.

They both looked at me, waiting for an answer. I stared out of the bathroom window. "Nah," I said. "Nothing's happened."

Jess glared at me through her clay-encrusted face. Even though I knew she was judging me, I didn't really care what she thought. And that's because I couldn't. The ground underneath me was about to collapse, and I was thousands of miles away from my family, my true friends. I was fucked because there was just so much darkness and rain. I was fucked because Portland was not the place that you would want to come apart. But it was exactly the kind of place that you would.

So, I sat in the bathroom with these two people. Really, it felt as if they were all that I had in the world except for Paul. And I knew that soon I might not have Paul anymore. He had become my safe base, my first real relationship person and without him in my life, I would again be that unsupervised kid with a key on a string, set loose in a scary world.

The three of us sat for a long time in the bathroom. We talked about me and Paul and Paul and Jess and her ex and Dana and her ex. We laughed so hard that we cried, while loud music played in the next room and heavy emotions and dense realities swirled around but never quite landed for long enough to become real.

At least that is what I told myself at the time.

* * *

I left the house and walked my bike down Alberta Street. I was not ready to go home to Paul, not wanting to continue the same conversation that happened every night. There was a gentle mist falling, and I was thankful for the light rain jacket that Paul made me buy before we moved to Oregon.

"They don't use umbrellas in Oregon," he had told me.

"Really? Then do you just get wet?"

"That's what I am saying, Ana. I'm saying people wear these hooded…"

We were at a sporting goods store in Manhattan's Union Square. It was the first time that I wondered if we were making the wrong decision to leave. I hadn't cried about leaving until that day, not until I looked at myself wearing one of those sporty jackets in the mirror. I didn't recognize myself and feared who I might become. I had never camped, never hiked, and never walked around in the rain willy-nilly without an umbrella. I took off the jacket, hung it back on the rack, and sat on the floor until Paul walked me out of the store, across the busy street and onto a park bench.

It was a hot summer afternoon, and Union Square was teeming with manicured office workers on their lunch breaks, nannies with multiples in strollers, and urban inhabitants with their small well-groomed dogs. I looked around and couldn't believe that my New York life was almost over—sitting in parks, walking in the streets, and taking in all of the vibrant energy that had fueled me since I was a kid.

"I don't want one of those ugly jackets," I told Paul as I sat with my head in my hands.

"How about we just get you one, and if you use it, you use it? If you don't, then you don't."

"Okay…"

I wasn't upset about the jacket that day; I wasn't ready to leave all that I had ever known. I was afraid of losing my identity as a city person with a cheap umbrella. Paul was ready to leave. He had already detached from the place where he grew up. He had already uprooted himself. He went back to the store and bought our jackets while I sat in the park and wiped away my tears with a flimsy deli napkin.

And now here I was thousands of miles away in Portland, wearing the jacket that we bought that day in Union Square. It felt like worlds away, and in so many ways, it was.

For a moment, I stood in front of a furniture repair shop that seems uninhabited, abandoned. There were a bunch of dusty tables, some broken chairs, and a few ripped up couches with stuffing spilling out of them like intestines. There was a big crack in the front window, and the floors looked like they hadn't been swept in decades. I saw no sign of people; it seemed as if the owner simply didn't return to keep shop, leaving people to wonder when they would get a call that their table or sofa was ready for pickup. I continued walking and passed a barbershop with the lights on and the ceiling fans spinning, but no customers were waiting their turn. The owner sat on a shiny red barber's chair, reading the newspaper and smoking a cigarette. Next door, there was a women's clothing shop that looked well-kept and orderly, but a closed sign was hung on the door.

There were many boarded up storefronts, and it was evident that the bones of these buildings were quite beautiful in the craftsman era. I could tell that Alberta Street was once a thriving commercial block, and maybe it could be again someday.

When I first moved to Milltown, I remember walking down Franklin Street, taking in all the shops, the cafes, the smells, and the people. I was forming a relationship to my new town. I would think about what it may have been like a hundred years ago—the same street, the same buildings, but different occupants from a former era. It felt like being a tourist in a European city for those first few months. It's the same feeling now in Portland.

But I now know that feeling would fade with time.

The day Paul and I were readying to make the cross-country trip out to Portland, my stomach knotted with anticipation and excitement. Dana had stopped by our apartment in Milltown, so she could toss a few boxes into the back of our U-Haul.

A few weeks prior to moving out west, I had gotten word from a mutual friend that Dana was also moving out to Portland. She hadn't worked at the club in a few months. It was one of those situations where someone doesn't show up for their shift and everyone whispers about what happened, and then they just don't come back again. I knew that she had broken up with her boyfriend, that they were notorious drunk fighters, and that maybe he was in a recovery program now. I knew that she was having a hard time. We hadn't been in touch for a few months, but I called her right away.

Dana told me that yes, she was moving out to Portland. But where I was ecstatic for the unknown newness and where I was excited about making such a huge life change, it felt as if Dana was running away from something. She sounded desperate and slightly manic. I knew she was running away from her ex and everything that comes with a recent breakup. But she did lighten up when she told me that Jess, an old friend of hers from high school, lived in Portland and had an extra bedroom that Dana would be taking. Dana said that Jess had also just broken up with a boyfriend.

"I think you'll like Jess," Dana told me.

"How long has she lived out there?" I asked.

"I think like a year."

I couldn't imagine what it would be like to live in Portland for a year. I couldn't imagine living anywhere but rat-ass Jersey.

On that glowing late summer afternoon while standing by the U-Haul, Paul and I were just about to give up on Dana. We were waiting for her to arrive so we could leave. We had already said our goodbyes to our family and friends and had many a bittersweet, alcohol and pot-infused goodbye party. Everything we owned had been methodically packed into a rented truck with Paul's old Subaru tethered to the rear.

Then around the corner came Dana in a borrowed car. She got out while clutching a cigarette, popped the trunk, and the three of us threw a few boxes into the back of our moving truck. Paul even had to bust out some packing tape because the boxes weren't even closed shut. Dana had plans to fly out the following week. She seemed sad, confused, and conflicted; there was a darkness surrounding her.

I felt like I was starting something new, while it seemed as if she was running away from something old.

We all said we'd see each other in Portland. But then I remembered that Dana had never even been to Portland before. She didn't even know what it would be like; she was going sight unseen. Paul and I had only spent a few days there, but we definitely had a sense.

"It's a cool place, Dana. You'll love it," I said as we hugged goodbye.

"Yeah, who the fuck knows," she said, trying to crack a smile.

Standing by the truck with the back still open, I waved goodbye to Dana as she drove away. I couldn't imagine what life would truly be like once we actually got to Oregon. Milltown had become the first home I had ever wanted to call home. And my people at Milltown Tavern were the only family that I felt truly saw me, truly accepted me. I knew that it was time to go. There was a need to flee in the pit of my gut that wouldn't make sense until it did.

I continued walking my bike down Alberta Street, passing a corner dive bar, the only pub on the street. There was a Help Wanted sign in the front window. I considered what it might be like to start bartending again. I might need to bartend again even though I had figured the long shifts, the drunken customers, and the inconsistent income were all things of the past. I couldn't imagine having the courage to put myself out there in that way again like I did when I asked for a job at Milltown Tavern. That was such a different time, and I was such a different person—naïve, immature, and unafraid. I was lucky to have landed that job, but I didn't realize it at the time.

I hopped on my bike and headed south toward the apartment that I shared with Paul. I was filled with unknown, uncertainty, and fear, but I kept going because there was nothing else that I could do. Because even when my shit fell apart, I just had to keep going.

Jersey

When I first learned how to bartend, it was at a chain restaurant called Bennigan's. It sat smack in the middle of a strip mall parking lot. I had worked there during my last year of high school and throughout my first few years of college. I managed to work my way up the bullshit corporate ladder from hostess to waitress to bartender. I was even awarded employee of the month at one point, which was the beginning of the end of Bennigan's for me. Everyone clapped as I sat there in my starchy shirt, peering down at the table. I knew that I couldn't play that dumbass fake role anymore—having to be nice to customers even though they were disrespectful, trying to upsell shit to people that they didn't need, and dressing in an ugly-ass uniform. I learned how to deal with assholes and how to pour a perfect beer, but then it started to reach the point where it was time to move the fuck on.

I had been driving into Milltown to take the train into Manhattan, trying to spend more and more of my free time away from the suburban pit of despair. I would go to the city alone to see independent films, and afterwards, I would perch on the Soho gallery docks or in the parks, drinking deli coffee and smoking Camel Lights. I would wander the streets, and I would sit on park benches for hours, observing people and eavesdropping on conversations.

And then one night, I was working a closing shift at Bennigan's. I was behind the bar, cleaning out the frozen margarita machine. The manager on duty was Pino, this Jersey-Italian guy with a wife, two little kids, and five girlfriends. He was sitting at the bar, counting out the register and drinking contraband margarita dregs out of a coffee mug.

"I got a bartending job in the city," I blurted out.

"What are you talking about, Ana? You know you can't work two jobs if you work here."

"Yeah, I know. I'm moving to Milltown. I have to find something closer," I told him.

All I really had to my name was three hundred dollars in cash and a lead on a basement room in a rundown apartment in Milltown. I didn't have a new job. I finished my side work, and Pino begrudgingly wrote up my two weeks' notice in the creepy back office. I picked up as many shifts as I could before handing in my crusty apron and walking out of there for the last time.

My family was not supportive of my impending urban transition; they wanted me to stay home and focus on finishing college. I did end up renting the room in the rundown apartment. It was two fifty a month, including utilities. A friend from high school and another friend of hers lived in the two upstairs bedrooms, and I would have the basement room. It was dark and moist down there, but I could walk to the train going into Manhattan, and that was enough. The previous tenant left behind a semi-habitable futon mattress, but other than that, all I had were clothes, books, and CDs. I had a car to get to class, and all I needed was a job.

I had spent some time at Milltown Tavern over the past few years. I had gone to see a few bands play but more just to meet up with friends from college. We would drink cheap red wine and smoke cigarettes at the café tables. Going to hang out in Milltown for the night was a way mellower version of going all the way into the city from the Jersey suburbs. I could still see the Manhattan skyline, and I didn't have to drive around for an hour, trying to find a parking spot. Milltown was this compact town with a vibrant urban pulse. There were tons of family-owned restaurants, bars, coffee shops, and boutiques lining Franklin Street, the main commercial avenue. There were pre-war brownstones and brick apartment buildings. It was as if a small chunk of Brooklyn had been extracted and placed on the river's edge in Jersey. Right in the heart of town was Milltown Tavern.

* * *

It was a bright afternoon in late May, right before Memorial Day weekend when a vast majority of the state of New Jersey hits the Garden State Parkway to head down the shore. I had just moved into Milltown. I had zero beach plans and only enough money for a few greasy slices of pizza.

My classes had just wrapped for the semester. I wasn't doing well in school because I had been too distracted by my ex-and-sometimes-not-ex boyfriend, Len. But I figured getting out of my mom's shithole apartment and into a shithole of my own would at least yank me out of my suburban Jersey depression.

My first stop in the job hunting mission was Milltown Tavern. It was my first choice of employment because the only other bars in town were either those dark open-during-the-day dive bars that cater to the local drunks or the too-brightly-lit sporty establishments better suited for the baseball hat wearing Wall Street types. I figured that I would just call Milltown Tavern and see if they needed a bartender. I didn't have a resume; I didn't need one back then. I either had legit bar experience of some kind, took one of those weird classes in the city, or just pretended to know what I was doing. I sat on the futon mattress, holding the cordless phone that I shared with my two roommates with a thin Milltown phonebook splayed out in my lap. I dialed the number. When someone picked up, I could hear running water and plates clanking in the background, so I knew it was the kitchen line from working at Bennigan's.

"Yeah. Milltown Tavern."

"Oh, hi. I was wondering if you guys needed a bartender," I said.

"No idea. Just come in and ask Rob," he said.

"Okay. When would—"

The guy hung up on me, so I turned off the cordless, shut the phonebook, and sat on the futon. There was a sharp pain in my stomach, and I felt like I might vomit. One of my roommates had some friends over, and they were playing loud techno music upstairs. The thumping bass made me feel even sicker. I knew that they had just driven back from a rave in Maryland, high on ecstasy, because they had walked into the kitchen with these huge perma-grins. Their big pants were all muddy at the cuffs from dancing around outside.

Meanwhile, I was eating a toasted bagel and brewing coffee while trying to be a real person in the real world.

I knew that living in that apartment would be temporary. I knew more than ever that I needed to pull my shit together to go see about that bartending job. I was down to my last few twenties and calling my dad for help would involve an epic lecture about moving out too soon, about focusing more on school, and about never making the right decisions.

How the fuck would I be able to actually talk face to face with Rob?

I had seen Rob a handful of times while hanging out at Milltown Tavern. A friend of mine, named Jen, was a DJ at our college radio station and had invited me to a few shows. She told me about Rob. I knew that she was hoping to land an internship at a record label after she finished school. She wanted to work for Lucky No. 7, the label that Rob's ran out of Milltown Tavern.

"Why don't you just ask Rob if you could help him with his label?" I had asked her.

"Because you don't just go up and talk to Rob," she snapped back.

We were sitting in the lounge area at Milltown Tavern. We were in these old stuffed chairs that I might find in my grandmother's living room, but these had been stained with wine and burned with cigarette holes. It was a slow weekday night, and the waitress with the giant bouffant hairdo who had served us drinks earlier was hanging out at the bar with her coworkers and hovering over the jukebox.

"That's him at the very end of the bar," Jen said.

"Who?" I asked

"The music guy. His name is Rob," she said.

I looked over and saw a tall guy with a shaved head who didn't look super young but didn't look super old either. I had definitely noticed him before. He had a presence, kind of like when I would see famous people in Manhattan. They had this glow, this magical presence. It was hard to explain, but it felt like that too with Rob. I could tell that everyone circled around him like he was at the center of something.

"What's his deal?" I asked Jen.

"Let's go for a walk by the river," she said.

It was the time of year when I felt that first chill off the Hudson River. I put on a pea green cardigan that I had found recently in a church thrift store. The Manhattan skyline was lit up, and I felt hopeful for the first time in a long time.

Things with the kind of ex-boyfriend were still super fucked up. I hung out with Len whenever he would let me, which wasn't very often. But classes had just started up again, and I was excited about this film studies class that I was taking.

Jen pointed up to a huge old brick building. She told me that was where the old paper mill used to be; this was why the town was called Milltown. The mill had opened in the early part of the century and then closed down in the seventies. Back then, the people who worked at the mill would go to Milltown Tavern after their shifts to drink. It was Rob's grandfather that owned the bar; it had been in the Farrelly family all these years, even though it had closed down for a while. After his grandfather passed away, Rob took over the bar and turned the back room into a music venue.

"How do you know all this?" I asked Jen.

"A bartender told me one night. She said the back room where the bands play was actually a speakeasy during prohibition."

By this point, Jen was annoying me with her boasting, spraying all kinds of knowledge and dropping names. I knew we wouldn't hang out anymore. This was how it was sometimes with friends from college. We'd be in a class together, see each other all the time, and start to hang out. But when our classes changed, we didn't see each other that much anymore. I knew that we would probably see each other in the quad and make half-ass plans to see a show, but those plans would never actually manifest. This seemed to be how it was when we weren't a fully formed people yet.

When I got home that night and walked into my mom's apartment, I knew it was time to go. I had spent way too many years of my childhood and adolescence in this apartment complex with the rest of the broke-single-mom kids. I had enough of seeing my mom in bed all the time: tired, depressed, and alone. She had never truly recovered from my father leaving her. And I was sick of her asking me for a twenty because she wouldn't get paid until the end of the week when it was supposed to be the other way around.

I was hoping for a message on my answering machine from Len and knew that I would drive over to his house if he wanted to hang out, even though it was well past midnight. But the red light wasn't blinking, so I just sat on my bed in the dark. The window was cracked a few inches to let in some of that cool fall air.

Maybe I'd move to Milltown in a few months. I'd get the fuck out.

Two

Portland

As I approached the house from across the street, I heard voices and laughter. The branches of the trees blew in the damp, cold wind as the leaves swayed, slapped, and dripped. I walked up the porch steps gingerly since it was quite dark and slippery. The only source of meager light was a tall white jar candle beside Jess and Dana who were sitting on an olive-green pleather loveseat. An open bottle of cheap red wine rested on the ledge behind them. We greeted each other with classic Jersey girl cheek kisses. I poured some wine into a coffee mug and sat with my back against the house as we passed around an American Spirit Yellow.

It was Friday evening, and all day, I had been looking forward to visiting with Dana and Jess. Paul was working late on a photoshoot, and I didn't want to go home to an empty apartment. I had just wrapped up the first week at my new job, my first job in Portland and my first job since leaving Milltown Tavern. I couldn't have been more content than sitting there with these two girlfriends: Dana, in her tight, ratty jeans and boy's hooded sweatshirt, had her dirty blond, short hair intentionally messy, and Jess, in her flowery vintage dress, black tights, and brown clogs, had her jet black bob with the severe bangs. Jess probably had the most Portland style, which was more cute girl vintage, because she had been there the longest, whereas Jess and I still ran our east coast just-out-of-the-nineties thrift store boy styles with our hair a bit rough and ratty. We still looked like we could be in an all-girl band.

It felt good being with them. The three of us grew up raw. None of us were privileged, and all came from a broken family system. There were no pretenses; we were comfortable being ourselves. It was that way sometimes when we came from the same place, grew up the same way. We sat in the quiet for a bit, smoking, sipping, and staring. I drank more wine and took a deep breath, relieved to be back at work finally and have a paycheck of my own on the horizon again. I was tired from starting a new job, meeting new people, learning new systems, and riding the waves of nervousness.

"Who are the guys that you work for again?" Dana asked.

"It's this guy Drew and another guy named Josh," I told her. "They were roommates in art school in California...and they moved to Portland after graduation to open up their own studio."

"Are they cool?" Jess asked.

"I mean, they seem pretty cool so far. Definitely a lot different than what we are used to back east, way mellower," I said as I passed the cigarette to Dana and took a sip of wine. "The whole thing actually feels like a sham. Like they are playing office or something."

"What do you mean?" Dana asked, taking a drag of the cigarette and laughing.

"I dunno. They come to work late in the morning, drink coffee, and cruise the net for like two hours before really doing anything. And Drew seems baked out of his mind most of the time. But it seems like they make pretty good money, so who knows."

"Is Paul friends with them?" Jess asked.

"I wouldn't say friends, but they could probably hang out."

We all heard the faint ringing of the phone. Dana jumped off of the couch and ran inside. A few moments later, she yelled to Jess that it was her mom. I sipped some wine.

As my body started to warm and as my nerves began to settle, I thought about the design studio and how I could never have imagined working at a place like that, how a place like that never even existed to me before. I never knew of a thrown together studio with dusty wide plank wooden floors and worktables made out of hollow doors and hobbyhorses. It had long floor to ceiling windows that clearly hadn't been washed in many years.

Well, in a way I had. It wasn't unlike the unconventional living space that Paul and his friends had crafted for themselves in Brooklyn. I thought about how there was something bohemian and appealing about the studio but also quite revolting as if I wanted to go there on a weekend and scrub away the grime. As if there was something underneath the surface that was dark, toxic, and unsettling.

I tucked my hands into my jacket sleeves, pulled my arms tight around my body, and took in the late autumn chill. The air is was filled with the satisfying aroma of a neighbor's backyard fire mixed with wet, decaying leaves and lingering cigarette smoke. The lights were now on inside the house, and I heard Jess talking on the phone. Dana came back out and resumed her spot on the couch.

"What's Paul doing tonight? Is he gonna come by?" she asked.

"Yeah, he'll be here soon, I think. He had to stop home after work to shower and change. Then he was gonna bike up."

"Is he glad you're working now?"

"Definitely. We've been strapped for cash. The move really cleaned us out. All our wedding money is gone, and we've been using credit cards for shit."

* * *

Paul had found me the job. Not long after we arrived in Portland, he started assisting a commercial studio photographer. During one of his first shoots, Drew and Josh had come in to get some apparel photographed for a client. At lunch, they all sat around and chatted. Paul gave them the rundown about how he had just moved out from Jersey with his wife, that things were going well so far but I needed to find some work. When Drew asked what kind of job I was looking for, Paul had said that I had recently been a bartender but I had also done some administrative work for the owner of the bar's record label, Lucky No.7.

"Wow! That's a killer label! It's the east coast version of Sub Pop pretty much," Drew said.

"Yeah, totally." Paul said.

Then Josh said that they might be getting a new client. They might be getting super busy and needed to hire someone to help keep things in check at the studio. He gave Paul their business card, a cut up vintage black and white photo on one side with a business name and phone number on the other. When Paul came home that evening, he was excited to tell me how he met these two cool guys who owned a design studio and how they might need some help. He handed me the card and told me to reach out.

"These guys are really chill, Ana. I think you'd like them," Paul told me.

“Blatant Design,” I said with a snobby tone, rolling my eyes as I looked at the half photo, half business card. “Yeah, okay. I’ll reach out.”

I was hesitant because I didn’t know if I had enough experience for what they needed. But I called the studio a few days later. Drew answered and was super quick on the phone. He told me to call back in a few weeks. By then, they’d know if they got the new client or not. I sat there thinking I wouldn’t call back. And right away, I called Paul at work, complaining that Drew seemed super ambivalent like I was bothering him. Like he just wanted to get off of the phone. Paul said that was how it was in Portland, that people were way more laid back, that he had been picking up on that vibe at work, and that it was something that we would need to get used to.

“They complain that I take things way too seriously,” Paul said about his coworkers.

“Really? You never told me that!”

“I mean, they say it in a joking way, but I think they… Wait. Sorry, Ana. I gotta run. Someone’s at the door.”

“Okay. Love you.”

“Love you too.”

When I told Dana and Jess about the possible job lead, it was as if they tried to be excited for me but seemed distracted, envious. We were at a coffee shop near their house, sipping muddy coffee and eating dry bagels. It was the only café in the Alberta Arts neighborhood, and even though it reeked of body odor and sugar, there was something oddly comforting about it. Bad art hung on the walls, and the staff was definitely high as shit but not as high as the patrons who spilled out onto the sidewalk with their chipped coffee mugs, patched clothing, and hand-rolled cigarettes.

They were kind of like the crusty street kids who hung out in Manhattan's East Village, but I could tell that these people weren't rich kids who had run away from their emotionless parents in Connecticut or Westchester County. They were legit dirty and threadbare, dreadlocked crusties that were clearly on some form of the Oregon welfare. Jess had said that some of them lived upstairs in single rooms and shared a bathroom. She had gone up there once to visit a painter friend, and when she went to use the bathroom, there was a tiny mushroom growing out of the side of the tub.

"Bukowski rooming house shit!" I said, laughing.

"Exactly. And a bunch of them live together in a big communal house down the block called The Clown House," Jess said, crossing her legs on the chair.

"Why is it called The Clown House?" I asked.

"Oh, because a bunch of them are performers, acrobats, and clowns maybe. I dunno."

One of the crusties rolled up on a super tall bike. I'd never seen anything like it. It was as if someone took a regular bike and stretched the frame to feel like it was a bike on top of a bike. He dismantled and bummed a smoke from a woman who was sitting on the sidewalk with her back against the café, reading a battered paperback. I watched her take a cigarette out of the pack, pull a lighter out of her front pocket, and light it for him as he hunched down inches from her face. That moment when someone lights a cigarette for someone else was just so intimate, so vulnerable to have a stranger that close. It was always so awkward for me.

We were sitting in the front window. A small splotch of sun fell onto the dark wooden table. Even though we didn't talk about it anymore, I felt a pang of hopefulness about this job prospect. I liked the idea of working at a graphic design studio and not at a bar. It wasn't a record label, I told myself, but maybe I would get some more marketing experience and then work my way back into the music industry.

"Do you think you'll get that job, Ana?" Dana asked, looking down at the table.

I looked at her and didn't know what to say. She had been sad and despondent these past few weeks. I knew she was still reeling from her recent breakup; she and Jess both were. And Jess was having such a hard time making ends meet in

Portland. She literally couldn't find anywhere to make money. They were both eternally broke and heartbroken. Even though they had each other, their friendship was clearly becoming strained. I could tell they were getting sick of being together, but in a lot of ways, they were clinging to each other because needed each other.

"I probably won't hear shit about that job again," I said, not wanting to make them feel bad and also convincing myself that I wasn't good enough.

"I bet you will," Dana said.

We sat quietly for a few moments.

At least Paul and I had each other. Even though money had been tight since we moved to Portland, I knew we would be fine. He was making decent money. Eventually, I would find a job, and we would be even better. We had some credit card debt from the move, but that would get paid off in time.

"Maybe we should just open up a coffee shop. We could have art shows and bands could play," I said, half-jokingly.

"That would be amazing!" Dana said, perking up. "Seriously though. The three of us have so much experience."

"Yeah, all we need now is a shit ton of money," Jess said, sarcastically.

"We'll find the money, Jess. I know a lot of people with money. People who would want to invest," Dana said, glaring at Jess.

"Okay. Then find us a bunch of money," Jess fired back.

"You guys, I was joking about opening up a coffee shop. Although, it is kind of a cool idea. Let's just talk about it another time," I said.

We refilled our coffee mugs, walked outside again, and took a seat on a wooden bench out front. It was a sunny and crisp fall day, not unlike a classic east coast autumn day but fundamentally different: the trees were different, the smells were different, and the light quality was different. I had heard that winter in Portland would be a steady stream of nonstop rain, so I looked up at the sky and drank in the small bit of sunny warmth that was offered that day. We sat quietly and drank our coffee before going our separate ways.

* * *

It was cold and damp when I walked outside late in the morning. The sky was a flat, muted gray. But the sun was trying desperately to peek through the clouds in a distance opening. It gave me a sense of hopefulness like maybe something good was about to come. "Could that be?" I asked myself.

Most days, I didn't know who I was or where I was anymore. I would wake up after Paul left for work, make a pot of coffee, eat some toast, and look for jobs. I called Dana, Jess, or both to see if they wanted to meet up. Sometimes, I would go for a late morning walk and look at all the beautiful, craftsman-style homes around our neighborhood. Maybe Paul and I could buy one someday. I would wait for Paul to get home in the evening, so we could make dinner together.

My universe had drastically shrunk since leaving Jersey. I would call my friends back east and tell them that everything was going well. I hadn't found a job yet but I would soon. Yes, Paul liked his job, and we were doing fine. We had a few friends, but we'd meet more in time.

I almost bailed on going to meet Drew and Josh. I kept telling Paul that they weren't even serious about hiring me, that I wouldn't have enough experience anyway, and that they were just meeting with me to be nice. And of course, Paul kept telling me to just go meet with them. Who knows what would come of it, but just go check it out.

"I don't know why you are freaking out, Ana. I mean, seriously. It's just an interview! Actually, it's not even an interview. You are just going to meet them, and maybe if they get that client, they might need some—"

"Yeah, I know. I know, Paul," I snapped. "It's just that I'm used to things being so much clearer, and people here are like whatever about shit. It's driving me fucking crazy to be…"

"I know. Me too, hon. But this is why we left Jersey. That's why came here, Ana. That's why we're here, and it's gonna take time."

I looked at Paul. Although I felt safe with him, something was just too much. He was my husband, and I loved him, but I had been torn away from my roots. Suddenly, in this new city, Paul sometimes felt like a stranger to me. I looked at him and saw a kind, adoring person with short, dark hair, brown eyes, and light skin. It was as if I had known him forever because he was so much like the guys I grew up with: the sharp Jersey wit and the fearless sense of humor.

He hadn't even been in my life for long at all. My only other longish relationship was with my high school slash college boyfriend, Len. Len was the opposite of Paul. It never seemed like Len gave a shit about me while Paul gave so much of a shit. I wasn't used to someone like that.

"Just go feel it out, Ana. It'll be good practice," he told me.

"If I can't find a job, I'll just move back home. You can stay here if you want," I said even though I didn't mean it.

"C'mon, hon. You're not going anywhere."

I parked on a leafy residential street, just far enough away from the studio that I could walk for a bit and check myself out in the rearview mirror. I took out my bobby pin and reset it, so that my hair was now out of my face. I reapplied dark red lipstick and checked my teeth. I had toiled over what to wear that morning and knew that I had to look good but not that good. This was a casual meeting with grubby graphic designers, so I decided on fitted jeans, a baggy vintage brown wool cardigan, a gray T-shirt, and a pair of Nike running shoes.

I walked up Southeast Belmont, past an old arcade and a used bookstore with shelves of paperbacks out front. I looked around and could feel the true essence of Portland: the vintage shops, the dive bars, and the street art. When I got to the building, I entered into a small vestibule littered with junk mail, and I pressed the buzzer that read Blatant Design. I got buzzed in a few seconds later, opened the second door, and made my way up a narrow, creaky stairwell that smelled like old coats.

I got to the second-floor landing and a door opened. A young woman in her early twenties approached. "Can I help you?" she asked.

"Oh, yeah. I'm here to meet with Drew and Josh," I said.

"Drew isn't here yet, but Josh is over there," she said, pointing to a tall guy that stared at a computer while wearing big puffy headphones.

"Thanks," I said and walked toward Josh. The young woman sat down at a desk in the front of the studio.

The studio was above a Middle Eastern restaurant, and it smelled of bread, spices, and mildew. It was this narrow room with high ceilings, long rows of desks lining two sides, and big floor to ceiling windows at the front of the space. I didn't want to bother Josh and felt like too much of a bother in this strangely quiet environment. In addition to Josh, there were three other people staring into giant computer monitors: one woman with long black hair, a guy wearing a big puffy jacket, a hat, and a scarf, and another super skinny guy with thick glasses and a plaid shirt. They all wore headphones and didn't turn to look at me as I walked past them.

"Hi, I'm Ana. Paul's wife," I said, standing beside Josh.

"Oh, hey. I didn't realize you were coming in," he said, pulling aside his headphones.

"Drew told me to come today," I said. My voice shook a little.

"No worries. He's not here yet, but let's go to the conference room in the back. He should be in any minute."

We sat at a big wooden table in a back storage room and spoke about what it was like living in Portland. I could feel my body starting to relax a little. Josh said he had moved to Portland a few years ago from California, and the city had already changed a lot. And then Drew appeared gripping a paper cup of coffee, saying he forgot I was coming in. I handed them each a copy of my resume, which I had fudged to appear way more experienced outside of bartending. I focused a lot of the bullshitting on my work with Lucky No. 7 records.

"So, what was it like working with all those amazing bands?" Josh asked right away.

"It was pretty cool," I said. "But it could be really stressful at times. Mostly just trying to get in touch with them, so they could make decisions." I said, laughing a little.

We talked about the process of producing a record. And then Drew and Josh would compare it to making a print ad or a catalog. There were similarities. I had worked with Rob long enough to at least see the process from start to finish a handful of times, so I was able to offer some input.

Although, throughout the conversation, I couldn't quite figure out what these guys were all about. I hadn't known anyone like them. They were a little older than me, close to thirty probably. Drew had this messy shoulder length blond hair and wore a T-shirt printed with an origami graphic. And

Josh was clad in a dark hoodie pulled over his head and some kind of vintage dress pants.

They reminded me a little of some of the West Coast bands that would come to play at Milltown Tavern, the rumpled musicians who had been sleeping in puppy piles in their tour van for weeks, months even. How they would come into the pub and collapse on the big couch, thankful for a pint and a band meal. When they found out that they could shower in the vacant apartment in the building next door, it was as if they might cry.

But Drew and Josh weren't broke, touring musicians. They were designers with relatively stable incomes.

"How do you guys know each other?" I asked.

"We went to college together. We were roommates for a while, and now we're kind of roommates again," Drew said, laughing.

"Cool," I said, laughing a little.

"Uh, yeah. We just got this new client and are about to get super busy. So, we'll probably need some help around here. We'll call you for sure after we figure a few things out," Josh said.

We made small talk about bands, Portland, and New York City before we stood up and shook hands. I walked down that dusty stairwell, figuring I would never hear from either of them again.

* * *

I was home with Paul one evening a few weeks after my meeting with Drew and Josh. We were making burritos and chatting in our small galley kitchen. He was talking all kinds of shit about his job. The photographer he assisted was an egomaniac, way worse than the guy he worked for in Manhattan. He said it was almost worse to have an inflated ego and not at least be from Los Angeles, New York, or San Francisco. The guy was a cheap ass. Paul was just realizing he was being underpaid and that maybe he should just start looking for another job.

"I mean, you could pretty much do whatever you want in Portland. Things you would never be able to do in New York," he said. His face was all red and sweaty.

"What do you mean?"

"Like people make all kinds of art and music, even though it's not that good."

I looked at Paul and was overcome by this feeling that I had made a mistake by marrying him, by moving all the way out west with him. He was still in his cycling clothing, tight Lycra shorts and a slim-fitting T-shirt. I was slightly repulsed by the way he looked and how he was talking. I felt like walking out of the apartment. He started going off about Jess and the low-rent artists she knew when the phone rang. I was thankful because Paul was on one of his negative tears. They really got me down. I had only just started noticing them once we got to Portland.

"Oh, hey. Is this Ana?"

"Yeah," I said.

"This is Drew from Blatant."

"Oh. Hey."

"Um, yeah. Do you think you come by the studio tomorrow to help us with a presentation?" he asked.

"Tomorrow? What time?"

"Come in around ten," he said.

"Okay," I said as my heart pounded in my chest.

The thought of going into that studio and jumping right into the fold made me feel as if my feet were no longer on the ground. I sat on a stool at the counter, while Paul took the burritos out of the oven. I could hardly eat. When I tried to talk to him about Drew asking me to go into the studio the next day, he went down yet another spiral about how flaky and unprofessional everyone in Portland is. That this would never happen in New York. I pretended to agree. We cleaned up, and then I tried to sleep.

I drove down to Southeast Portland the next morning and started going into the studio on weekdays after that.

Mostly, I went out for coffee and lunch runs for the designers. I answered the phone, tended to the shipping and receiving, and chatted a lot with the UPS guy. It wasn't amazing work, but I was happy to have a job that didn't involve pouring beers and staying up until dawn. I liked getting up in the morning and having a sense of purpose.

By the time I had left Milltown Tavern at the end of the summer, I was jaded as fuck. I couldn't open a Rolling Rock for another needy person. Even though I had been learning a lot from working at the label with Rob, it got hard to go down to the dingy basement office and not know if I would get either berated or highly praised for my work.

Although I hadn't worked with Rob and the label for long, I learned a shit ton. Mostly, I learned how to deal with people and not in a someone-needs-a-drink way but in a semiprofessional-making-a-proper-phone-call way. I would arrive at the office downstairs from Milltown Tavern around noon a few days a week and stay down there until I had to open up the bar. Rob would run up and down the stairs all day, vacillating between the office phone and the bar phone, placing food and alcohol orders, and talking to musicians about either booking shows or recording an album. He would give me some tasks, mostly to make calls around scheduling musicians to record, bookings for studio time, pressing album production details, and things like that. Grunt work.

If I knew Rob would be upstairs for a while, I could get into a good flow, and it gave me a lot of fulfillment. When he had one of those days where he would breeze in and out in a manic state, it was hard to focus. I knew I could fuck something up, and he could freak out on me.

But I grew up like that. My stepmother was that brand of volatile; it was familiar, and I put up with it most days. It gave me hope that someday I could maybe work a legit career job; it made me feel like I had a purpose. I never felt hope before really, and I never felt like I had a purpose. I found that I was good at talking to people, good at organizing details, and good at communicating back to Rob what I figured out. He never told me, but I knew that he liked my work and that was a lot for me.

* * *

After my first day at the studio, I wanted to go straight to Jess and Dana's to drink wine, smoke, and share my excitement with them. But I knew that Jess would be too envious, and

Dana had been in such a dark place lately that she wouldn't be able to be happy for me. Jess was making just enough to cover rent and food. Maybe some of her bills got paid, and Dana was struggling hard to find any work at all. Rent and food were pretty cheap, and there were affordable art studios, but making a living wage was another story altogether. It seemed as if the artists began fleeing too-expensive San Francisco, New York, and Los Angeles for ultra-accessible Portland. They took all of the flexible-style jobs.

It was hard to witness Dana's struggles. I wanted to tell her to stick it out, something would shift, and she would find something, but I could tell she couldn't hear what I was saying. Her eyes would glaze over, and I could feel the weight of her darkness.

Thinking about Dana and Jess and their ongoing struggles made me feel grateful that I didn't have to resort to pouring drinks or waiting tables again. But even though I had a decent job and a supportive husband who also had a decent job, there was still this constant ache in my heart.

I already missed Milltown Tavern and my people from there. I missed living near Manhattan. I daydreamed about the train rides that had carried me under the Hudson River and spit me into a city that I loved like an actual person. I missed all of my friends, and I kind of missed my family, but in a really deep place, as deep as the core of my being, I missed where I came from.

What soothed me is that I had a job and Paul, and maybe, in time, we would find our way back east again. That's what got me through the days: the fact that this Portland experiment was temporary.

* * *

During one of my first days working at the studio, Drew had me organize the contact list on his computer. I was still kind of jittery about going to work in the mornings and didn't really know what my role was once I got there. Everything was unfamiliar: how quiet it was, how coworkers hardly spoke to each other unless there was a reason, and how tasks took such a long time.

I mostly sat at a small desk close to the drafty front door unless I asked anyone if they needed help, coffee, or food. I had to find ways to stay busy. There was always so much to do at Milltown Tavern. We never sat around unless we were taking smoke breaks or taking turns standing in the back of the band room, catching a song or two from the show. But this was the kind of job where I had to somehow find things to keep me busy, which was something I certainly wasn't used to.

"Wait. Is this Jim Lancer from Kinnelon, New Jersey?" I asked Drew, sidling up to his desk with his contact list.

"Yeah, totally. We were roommates in college," he said like it was no big deal that I knew this person.

"That's crazy! He's good friends with one of my friends from back home. They grew up together," I said.

"Crazy. Small world," Drew said before turning back to his computer screen.

"This guy is so mellow," I said to myself. I was freaking out that we had a common friend, but he had hardly reacted. I remembered what Paul said about how people in Portland were super mellow. Maybe this was a good thing, a better thing. I was constantly worried about fitting in, how we might stick out too much for being these feral east coast types. There was definitely something I really liked about Drew's chill attitude. It was a bit awkward at times, but there was also something calming about it.

When I got back to my desk, I sat there, thinking about Jim Lancer from Jersey and all my old friends. I thought about my mother who was depressed and in bed all day but could fly off the handle out of nowhere. I thought about my father who was either happy-go-lucky or overly demanding, depending on how much he had to drink or what mental state my stepmother was in. I thought about my older brother who could be removed from what was in front of him and how he mostly chose to escape from the hard things. My sister had her own life. She was busy managing a household—a husband and two young kids. But my brother, who was the closest in age to me even though he was ten years older, had become my anchor because all of the other adults in my life were way too fucking unpredictable.

I thought about how my family had given me such a hard time for leaving. They couldn't see it as a good thing. They saw it as me dicking around again like I had in college. They saw it as yet another lack of focus. Again, I was a flake.

After I cleaned up Drew's contact list, which took all of ten seconds, I had a coffee and waited for someone to give me something to do, feeling super uncomfortable about just sitting around. I began to wonder if I had made the right choice by moving out west.

Paul was my family now. We were married, even though we had only known each other for a few years. Really, we were just getting to know each other. He was kind, and he adored me, but he could also be emotionally unstable. We both had such hard times as kids. Now everything and everyone we had ever known was back in Jersey, and we were together, alone in this new life.

Drew saw that I needed something to do, so he sidled up next to me and showed me how to access some client files on the computer. This way, I could start getting a sense of the work they did. We ended up chatting more about Jim from Jersey, and something about that connection made it easier to be around him. The rest of the designers hardly spoke, and Josh was always on the phone with clients.

“How do you and Paul like it out here so far?” Drew asked.

“It’s cool. We have a few friends here that we knew from Jersey, but we’ll find more people to hang out with eventually.”

“Yeah. It can take a while out here. People have their little bubbles.”

“Do you like it?” I asked him.

“Yeah, I do.”

Drew had to answer a client call, so I rooted around with some of the files that he had shown me: mostly photo-driven snowboarding ads, some illustrated posters, and T-shirt graphics. It reminded me of being a preteen and pouring over skateboarding magazines alone in my room, how I would dream of living in those sunny places where I could surf and skateboard all year round.

Being in the studio made me feel connected to something again, like when I started hanging out with skateboarders back in Jersey. We would hang out for hours at someone’s backyard ramp or maybe get a tip on an abandoned backyard pool. We would catch a ride into the city to go to the Brooklyn Banks or Washington Square Park. I was the girl with the big army pants and the half shirt, sitting on the curb and rolling around once in a while on a borrowed board.

That was the first time in my life I truly felt like I was a part of something. The first time I felt like I actually fit in somewhere.

* * *

After a few weeks of working at the studio, Drew and I started going out to lunch or coffee. Sometimes, Josh would join or maybe one of the other designers. It really hit me that things took so much longer in Portland. Back in Jersey, relationships were so transparent and in my face. I got to know people right away, and either I liked them, or I didn't. Even waiting for food or drinks took longer in Portland. People drove slower, walked slower, and spoke slower. Everything seemed to have a lag time like everyone was stoned, and most of them probably were.

Drew invited Paul and I out to a bar after work one night. We met at this dark, windowless, hole-in-the-wall dive bar that looked like it had been extracted from a creepy 1970's movie set. It stunk of stale beer and cigarette smoke, and there was this oddball mixture of old pepper-nosed drunks sipping brown liquor and twenty and thirty-something hipsters drinking cheap canned beer. Nothing in between. Paul and I walked in, sidled up to the bar to grab drinks, and looked at each other.

"This place is trippy," Paul said to me.

"I know. I kind of like it."

We found Drew sitting at a corner table with a handful of guys. He introduced us. They were mainly snowboarding industry friends, all of them recent Oregon transplants. One tall skinny guy with shaggy brown hair had grown up down the Jersey shore. A couple of them had just moved from Vermont.

I sat next to Drew while Paul chatted with the Jersey guy about what beaches they grew up going to. I was quiet because we were broke and could only stay for one beer. I hadn't gotten my first paycheck yet, and Paul's paycheck had already gone to rent, bills, and food.

Drew got up and came back with a round of beers. I knew we wouldn't be able to reciprocate. That truly put me in a shame state, reminiscent of being a broke kid going to school without lunch money.

I tried to engage in a conversation that Drew was having with his friend, a snowboarding photographer, about an upcoming trip that the guy was taking to California, but I felt like I had nothing to offer. I just listened, smiled, and nodded. It wasn't that I was uncomfortable being around a table of guys since so many of my closest friends were guys. It was more that I felt lesser again.

After I finished that second beer, I got up and put my jacket on. I could tell that Paul didn't want to leave; he enjoyed talking to the Jersey guy, but he got up too. We said we had to head out. Everyone sort of waved goodbye. Drew said he'd see me on Monday. Paul and I left the dark bar.

"I feel really bad that we couldn't buy a round of beers," I said to Paul as we walked to the car.

"I bet Drew doesn't give a shit. He doesn't seem to give a shit about anything."

I was quiet in the car all the way home. I was reminded too much of growing up with an eternally broke mom. I knew it would take a while to get back on our feet after spending so much money to move across the country. Paul and I had talked about it many times. We knew everything would be okay after a few months. It was part of the plan, and it didn't bother him like it bothered me.

"My mom was really good at stretching food and money until payday," Paul had told me after we first met.

"Really?"

"She made shitty money working in the school system, and we hardly had any money from my father's pension, but she made it work somehow."

"That's completely opposite of my mother. If she had money, she spent it. If we didn't have enough food in the house, we didn't eat, or she had to borrow money. It was fucking humiliating when she had to go begging for help. I hated it," I said.

"That's really sad, Ana."

Even though I fretted about it all weekend, when I got to the office the following Monday, Drew never mentioned anything about the beers or about us leaving so abruptly. He just said it was cool hanging out with me outside of work. I felt relieved, and all the shame melted away in an instant.

I invited Drew to a potluck dinner at Dana and Jess's the following week. I had been considering setting him up with Jess for a while but wasn't sure if either of them would be into it. Jess had just found out that her ex-boyfriend was dating someone else. She was pining for a date to get her mind off of things, and I figured Drew could be a good option. He was definitely single and told me that he hadn't been with anyone in a while. He briefly mentioned a German girl he was messing around with for a few months, but she moved back to Europe. He also had asked out some skater girl recently, but she never got back to him.

"He's the catch of the century," I had told Jess a few days earlier while she was brooding about her ex.

She had been driving Dana crazy with her moods. Well, they had been driving each other crazy with their moods.

"What do you mean 'the catch of the century?'"

"It's just that he owns his own business and his own house, and he's pretty cute," I told her.

We were scrappy Jersey girls, and the only dateable guys we knew around our age maybe had okay jobs, but there was no way they owned their own business or homes. If they were lucky, they owned their own car. The only men we knew who owned their own businesses or houses back home were old, bald, and married.

When I talked to Drew about it, he said he was open to meeting Jess, and Jess said that she was open to meeting Drew. We basically concocted this slapdash dinner party.

* * *

On a weekday evening the following week, I met up with Drew outside of Jess and Dana's. I brought cheese and bread, and Drew brought chips and salsa. Mostly everyone else brought hummus, and there was a lot of cheap wine on the table. Jess invited a handful of artist friends from the neighborhood. We introduced ourselves around informally. There was a longhaired guy sitting on the couch, fiddling with some chords on an acoustic guitar. A Duraflame was burning in the fireplace.

About five of us sat around the dining table, picking at food, sipping wine, and talking about semi-important things. There was a pretty brown-skinned woman with long dreadlocks talking to a skinny shaggy-haired guy about their time at Bard College. At one point, Drew left my side to chat with Jess in the small galley kitchen. They had avoided each other for the first part of the night. Jess seemed nervous about the set up, and so did Drew. I could tell that Jess had made an effort in getting ready for the evening. Her blunt cut, black hair was perfectly straight, and she had put on a vintage dress with black tights and cowboy boots. The house was the cleanest I had ever seen it too.

I was relieved when Dana arrived home from helping the next-door neighbor with some house projects, probably scraping and sanding cabinet doors which was something she had been doing for the past few weeks. It was her only source of income, and it was meager. She sat down across from me, winked, poured herself a glass of wine, and gnawed on a piece of crusty bread. Neither of us wanted anything to do with the liberal arts college talk.

But then Dana glanced into the kitchen and noticed Drew talking to Jess before looking at me with a funny expression across the table. "Who the fuck is that?" she mouthed.

"It's my boss," I mouthed back, laughing.

Something shifted in me. I suddenly felt sick to my stomach, so I put my glass of wine down. The guitar guy played "Closer to Fine" by the Indigo Girls, and a couple of people sang along. I felt so warm that I got up to go outside for air.

Dana stood up and followed me out to the porch with an American Spirit pack in her hand. "I bet you'll leave Paul for that guy," she said, passing me a cigarette and laughing.

"Wait. What? Why would you say that?"

"Cause you didn't like Jess talking to him," she said, inhaling and blowing smoke out of the side of her mouth.

"Really? I didn't? What do you mean?"

We both started laughing hysterically. I kept asking Dana why she would say something so crazy. She kept telling me I looked jealous when Jess was talking to Drew. That was all she could say. We finished our cigarette and headed back into the house to sit by the Duraflame. We listened to bad music and smart people talking about dumb things.

Jersey

The side door creaked when I opened it. Even though I had walked through that door so many times before, it was solely for shows or to meet up with friends. This time was different. It was daytime, and both the bar and the restaurant areas were lit with natural light. There was no clanking of glasses, and no loud conversations over loud music. The black spongy kitchen and bar mats were in a pile by the bathroom. The wooden café chairs were stacked upside down on the tables, and the ceramic tile floors wet from a recent mopping. The air was dense with prep cooking and pungent cleaning solution.

I felt nerve-rattled, like an intruder. It was as if I had no business being in such a sacred space.

I wore a tight black T-shirt and even tighter boys Levi's cords in crayon red and thick heeled, black boots. I reeked of day-old Egyptian Musk. Rob stood at the end of bar, holding a yellow legal pad with lots of pages folded back. He had a pen stuck to the top of one ear, and a phone was pinned to the other. The long, curly phone cord stretched all the way from the middle of the bar, and a cigarette burned in a clear glass ashtray next to him. I knew he was doing the ordering from working at Bennigan's. The managers would shuttle in and out of the back office, carting around stacks of order forms and binders.

I stood in the middle of the café area with my heart racing, pretending to look at some of the artwork hung on the walls. There were large, colorful, abstract paintings, and there were a few framed graphic concert posters.

Rob walked behind the bar and put the phone back on the handset. "Can I help you?" he asked.

"I called earlier to see if you needed a bartender. The guy—"

"Do you know how to pour a beer?" he asked nonchalantly.

"Oh. Yeah," I said.

He took a long drag of his cigarette, blew out a plume of smoke, and gestured to follow him behind the bar. He handed me a thick glass mug from the sink drain and told me to pour a beer. We stood next to each other at the long beer pulls. I was about a foot shorter than Rob and was definitely intimidated by his stature, his presence, and his reputation. I angled the mug to the Bud tap and poured the beer with just the right amount of foam. I set the beer down over a bar napkin.

He picked it up and poured in down the drain. "Come in at four on Thursday. Someone will be here show you around," he said, taking one last drag of his cigarette and stomping it out in the ashtray.

"Come in here to work?" I asked.

"Someone just left to go on tour with his band, and we're short a bartender," Rob said. "What's your name?"

"It's Ana."

"Okay, little miss Ana Banana. I'm Rob," he said, grabbed his notepad, and walked toward the back of the room and down a set of stairs.

I stood by the empty bar for a few moments in some kind of shock. I was startled by someone rustling around in the kitchen, so I walked out the door and onto Franklin Avenue. I headed toward the shit part of Milltown, past the old Italian men sitting on folding chairs, the corner deli, the dry cleaners, and the brownstones with their big stoops. I went through the park with the screaming kids, the barking dogs, the pizzeria, and the hot dog vendor on the corner.

When I got closer to my apartment, I ran down the block because I was fucking beside myself.

It had been a few weeks since I moved to Milltown. The apartment was cheap, big, and broken down, which was fine, but the main concern on my end was the roommate situation. They played copious amounts of techno music, wore oversized pants and thick-heeled shoes, and painted on shit tons of glitter makeup. The real actual fucking concern was that they took ecstasy like it was Flintstone vitamins and spent all of their free time either going to raves, planning on going to raves, or talking about how they went to past raves.

But my roommates were gone a lot, and I would be working at Milltown Tavern. So, fuck it. I'd live there for a few months until something better came along with less eternally dancing roommates. This new job could be a way out of the incessant techno beats.

It was super sunny and warm out, the first hit of urban summer. In the years to come, I would learn that there was nothing quite like the feeling of that initial warm hit of summer in the city. There was this overall sense of manic energy in the air. I made it to the ass end of town and turned the corner, practically skipping down my block while consumed with so much hopefulness. Cars pumped with bass, and little kids wandered around in diapers. People spilled all over the sidewalk really. It was noisy as fuck on that block, and I found how there were people around all day, all night beautifully comforting. What I liked was that nobody was ever alone. I grew up so alone all the time. All I had ever wanted was to look out the window and see life happening.

When I walked inside and up the stairs into the kitchen area, it was dark and hot, and it smelled like weed. Both bedroom doors were shut, which meant my roommates were still sleeping. I hadn't witnessed them awake before three in the afternoon since I moved in. When I went back down to my basement, my roommate's boyfriend, a prematurely balding, pale-skinned dude who probably hadn't seen the sun in over a decade, was spinning ambient records on two big turntables and huffing on a tall, colorful bong. He had giant spongy headphones on and was prancing around behind the table. I had slowly been realizing that this guy didn't pay rent but basically lived in our apartment. I went into my room and shut the door.

But I didn't know what to do with myself. I was dying to tell somebody about the new job, but I was freaking out too much. I considered calling my brother. He had helped me move in, and when we drove down to where my apartment was—way past all the nice brownstones and the leafy parks and toward the abandoned buildings and the thumping bass—he looked around and couldn't believe that I was actually going to live in that dumpy apartment. He had been living in a nice neighborhood in Queens, not far from where we had lived as kids before our parents split up. He felt bad for me; I could tell that he was concerned. He wanted to give me advice, but he also knew it was too late. I wouldn't listen anyway. He just kept telling me to be careful at night.

My nerves were on fire; my stomach was a pile of acid. What the fuck would I wear to work on Thursday? Of course, the sweaty, premature balding guy was still playing that painful music, and the bong smoke was now wafting under my door. The last thing I needed was contact high, so I walked back upstairs, sat on the front steps, and smoked a Camel Light.

The neighborhood was alive. A Chihuahua with a giant tumor hanging from its belly walked by unattended. Two older gentlemen sat on folding chairs, playing cards with a small radio nested beside them. I wanted to be nowhere else in the world. I sat for a while, thinking about what kind of summer was ahead of me.

I would probably make some decent money at Milltown Tavern. I could probably buy some nice shit to wear to work. I could afford to spend more time in the city, seeing films at the Angelika and eating something other than dollar pizza slices and bagels.

I finished my cigarette and went inside to call my brother.

Three

Portland

It was a Friday evening, and a bunch of us from the studio had gone to a bar after work. I invited Paul to join, but he was too tired from a long week of dealing with difficult clients. He had been complaining a lot about his coworkers, about his clients, and about how everything took forever in Portland. It was starting to wear me down. When he would bring things up, I would nod, and he would unload and wouldn't stop until I told him to stop.

"I don't know what the fuck is up, but Paul keeps bitching about people he works with," I said to my friend, Mark, over the phone. He was back in Jersey.

"You shouldn't have gotten married, Ana," Mark said, laughing. "You can't just return him because he's a little defected."

"Maybe he needs to see a shrink. Anyway, what's the scene over there?" I asked.

Mark went into an hour-long rant about how Rob was talking about selling Milltown Tavern. How some rich-ass businessman from the suburbs wanted to buy it and turn it into a brewery. How Rob kept talking about how Milltown was spoiled now. How it had changed too much in the past few decades. How he didn't know how long bands would actually want to play there anymore.

I tried to catch Mark up on life in the wild, wild west, saying that I was actually starting to enjoy my job, that I was meeting more people, that Dana was struggling to get by, and that I wasn't sure if she was going to stay in Portland. But Mark was too fired up about Milltown Tavern to focus on what I was saying.

"Dude, it would be awful if he sold the club," I said.

"Tell me about it. It would be the end of a fucking era."

"Listen, I gotta go. But say hi to everyone. And who knows? Maybe I'll come back. Maybe Paul will go postal, and I'll have to put him away."

When I got off the phone, I wanted to crawl into a hole and hide. The thought of Milltown Tavern closing broke my heart to bits. Fuck. Fuck. Fuck. I missed everyone so much. I even missed Rob. When I left to move out to Portland, he was aloof with me, but he gave me a big kiss on the cheek and told me I could come back anytime.

* * *

The bar was crowded and loud with the cracking of pool balls. Everyone else from the studio had already left and gone home. After who knows how many beers and way too many cigarettes, Drew and I were both pretty hammered. Neither of us wanted the night to end, but we both wanted to get the fuck out of that bar. Evening happy hour at a dark and dingy dive bar in Northeast Portland was one thing, but the night crowd was another. The jukebox played classic rock, which became super irritating. Drew said we could walk to his place to smoke a bowl.

"Okay," I said.

While he was in the bathroom, I thought about how Drew and I were at Jess' potluck only a few weeks prior. Jess was bummed to see us leaving. We talked about it a few days later, so I knew she thought Drew was pretty attractive. He *was* attractive. And he had his shit together. But Drew was ambivalent about Jess. I didn't think he could take her seriously. Maybe it was because she worked as a waitress and hocked subpar hobbyist art on the side.

I had seen this kind of art snobbery at Milltown Tavern. Certain people were not taken seriously because maybe they hadn't reached a certain level of recognition. If they did not have a "deal" of some sort, whether it was a published book, a record contract, or a gallery show, they weren't a proper artist. I remember feeling like I could never even attempt to launch into art myself. I had zero confidence even though I dabbled in various art forms throughout college: pottery, life drawing, and photography. I even submitted a short story to a literary journal, and when they rejected it because the deadline had already passed, I took it as failure.

After about a twenty-minute walk, we arrived at Drew's house. It was close enough to Alberta Street and not that far from where Jess and Dana lived, but it was in a bit of a sketchy neighborhood. He had told me that he heard gunshots from time to time, that he often witnessed drug deals, and that someone had been murdered on his front lawn years ago. But his house was a sweet old bungalow, and even though it wasn't in the best shape, it was quite charming. It seemed like the kind of place where babies were born in the kitchen, where I'd cook big pots of soup and raise a family. There were these amazing hardwood floors, chunky molding, and built-in bookshelves. But Drew lived with another guy, and they clearly didn't give a shit about keeping it clean. It was a little dusty, and it was pretty messy. Piles of shit were everywhere.

"So, do you think you want to hang out with Jess again?" I asked Drew.

"Nah."

"You just not into her?"

"Yeah, I don't think we have a lot in common," he said.

I could tell that he didn't want to get into it, and I didn't probe any further. We were still pretty buzzed, and I didn't want to say things I would regret later.

We decided to watch old skateboard videos on VHS from back when he skated with our common connection friend, Mike from Jersey. But the footage started mid tape. It showed a bunch of dudes drinking beers in a shitty bright kitchen and zapping each other with a stun gun. They were clearly wasted and laughing hysterically. In another scene, one guy plays William Tell and puts an apple on top of his head, and another guy shoots at it with a BB gun. Complete shenanigans. It cut to the bright desert sun: a bunch of skateboarders in and around an empty backyard pool.

Even though the landscape was different, the skateboarding, the cheap watery beer, and the tomfoolery were familiar. I had spent many youthful Suburban Jersey afternoons in similar habitats, relishing in the freedom of the long carves on spongy fat wheels. The joy of leaning into a turn and feeling a light breeze through my hair that would blow away all the vile and the stink of my life back at home. It made everything seem like it was going to be okay. Having shit tons of fun and being with friends always made me forget about all the sucky parts in my life, for a little while.

As I sat in this funky old house and in a strange new city, it was as if I was watching my own past come into the present. Even though Drew was profoundly different than the people I grew up with, his disposition was so calm and easy. There was also something eerily familiar about him. As we got to know each other more and more each day, sometimes working side by side for hours at the studio, it seemed like he was more like the friends of my Jersey youth.

I felt nostalgic and emotional, and I was still warmly buzzed. “I’m so glad we’re friends,” I mumbled to Drew. “Can I hug you?”

I didn’t wait for a reaction. I just dove into him. We hit the wooden floorboards in front of his television, making a pile on the ground. The tape still rolled on the screen with the carving on the sides of the pool and the hooting of the bystanders. I did not think of Paul the whole time our bodies remained entangled with his long blond hair in my face. I did not think about being married to another person. My lips found Drew’s, and the physicality of the space we inhabited took over.

That is until the VHS tape came to a stop, and the screen went blue.

* * *

By the time I left Drew’s and walked toward my apartment in the cold rain, I was sober and sad. I was in complete shock; my head buzzed with details of how the evening unfolded and how Drew was now this other kind of person to me, not just this guy I worked with.

There had been lunches alone with him. The walks to get a late afternoon coffee. One night, he even stopped by our apartment and ended up hanging out with me and Paul. The three of us smoked weed, played music, and shot the shit. When Paul went to crash out, Drew and I stayed up chatting until he was sober enough to get himself home.

When Paul woke up that next morning, he acted strange while we were sitting at the kitchen table and drinking coffee. He read the paper and didn't talk much. He must have known that my feelings for Drew had taken root. But he also knew I spent so much of my youth and adulthood glued to close guy friends.

* * *

When I got to the apartment, it was dark inside, but the streetlights cast an ominous glow. I could see where I was going, but there was a chill up my spine from the creepy stillness of the nighttime unknown. It had to be past three in the morning, and I was already hung over. I shook Paul awake and told him everything that had just happened between me and Drew in one fast, narrative stream.

Paul opened his eyes, but he didn't say anything. I sat on the edge of the bed while he stared at the ceiling. I remembered how we were a year ago, wondering how we could get back there. How he had come into Milltown Tavern one night and how we had recognized each other from college. How we exchanged numbers and met up the following week. It didn't take long to realize we were going to be more than just friends. After our second time hanging out, we made out under an old tree in Milltown and pretty much spent every night together after that. We had pushed fast-forward. We had gone from dating to living together to getting married to moving all the way across the fucking country in under two years.

"I knew you had feelings for that dude. I could tell from how you were acting that night he came over," Paul said after a long pause.

"But I didn't even know," I said, crying hysterically.

"C'mon, Ana. I'm not stupid, and neither are you."

We didn't talk much. I cried a lot, and Paul held me. Somehow, we fell asleep. But I woke up a few hours later with a splitting headache and feeling like a cheating asshole failure. Of course, I would manage to fuck up the only stable thing that had ever happened to me, and I would hurt the only person who was willing to not only commit to being with me but who was willing to marry me. I always felt like a total fuck up and kissing this person, my boss for fuck's sake, truly validated what a loser I was.

I remained in bed next to Paul and made a running tab of all my shortcomings. I was a good student, placing in advanced classes. But after my parents split up, my dad remarried, and my mom went nuts, I did super shitty in school. I got bad grades through high school, and I somehow managed my way into a state college. But it took me six years to get a dead-end philosophy degree. I hung out with sketchy kids in my apartment complex after school, and we would sometimes get drunk. I always tried to make out with one guy or another even though I knew they would reject me. I pressured my first high school boyfriend to have sex before he was ready. The only other legit relationship I ever had besides Paul consisted of too many years of drunk fighting at house parties and never knowing if we were together or not. I never had enough money to make ends meet on my own. My rent and bills were always late. I was known as a super flake by my friends because I would break plans last minute or leave parties without saying goodbye.

I pretty much always felt that people were eternally disappointed in me.

I thought about how Paul came along and how my life stabilized after we got together. I finally had everything I didn't have as a kid, but now it was clear that all those things would never be enough for me.

* * *

When I got to the studio, Drew hadn't arrived yet. Josh was on the phone at his desk, and the other designers were arriving one by one in complete silence with their messenger bags slug over their shoulders. I sat at my desk and nursed a coffee for most of the morning.

I felt like total shit. I wanted to run away. I wanted to book a plane ticket back home to Jersey, so I could be with my people. I figured that I would just quit working at the studio. I had thought about it all weekend, which meant two full days of Paul not wanting to talk about anything. I figured I would give the proper two weeks' notice and then chalk up that make out session with Drew as a dumb, drunken mistake. I would move on from this job and focus on my life with Paul. We needed my income, but I could always find a temporary bartending job if it came to that.

Maybe screwing around with Drew was a sign that I had to go, that this job was a giant boring waste of my time.

I began crafting a formal resignation letter to Drew and Josh. But the UPS guy arrived and messed up my flow. I was signing off on a package when Drew walked by my desk. I looked up and saw his face was scraped up and encrusted with blood. One pant leg was rolled up over the knee. He didn't say anything to anyone. He just went to his desk near the big window and fired up his computer.

"What the fuck, dude?" Josh said, swiveling in his chair to face Drew's desk.

"What?" Drew said.

"You're all banged up. You're bleeding."

"Oh, I stopped at Burnside on my way in for a skate and bailed really hard."

I considered ignoring the situation, but instead, I went to the bathroom and got stack of wet paper towels. I took some antibiotic ointment and bandages from the first aid kit before walking over to Drew's desk. We didn't say anything to one another, but I could feel him pining for my attention. I knew this from spending a lot of time around skateboarders. They acted all distant and tough when they got hurt, but they would cry if nobody else was looking. It had something to do with their upbringing, that there was a deep inner need to be nurtured no matter how old they were. Drew was hurt pretty bad but not hospital bad. I wasn't sure what he wanted, but I knew he needed something, so I helped him clean up his wounds.

"You wanna maybe grab lunch in a bit?" I asked impulsively. My heart raced.

"Uh. Yeah. Sure," Drew answered.

I went back to my desk and worked on my resignation letter. I figured I would tell Drew that I was leaving over lunch, and then we would circle back with Josh. I would tell them both that the job wasn't a good fit for me. I felt good about things for a few fleeting moments. But then it hit me super hard that I had truly hurt Paul. He had been good to me. I couldn't imagine living without him. Yes, he was my husband, but he had also become my best friend, and he literally held me together by some damaged seams.

It made me sick to think about what he must have been feeling. He had shut down over the weekend and wouldn't let me comfort him. I wanted to call and check in, but I knew we couldn't talk until later that evening since he was busy with a photo shoot. I went to the bathroom and cried.

When Drew and I walked out onto the street to grab lunch at a nearby cafe, I looked up into his blue-gray eyes, and I felt something that I had never felt before. It was something that rattled me from the inside and shot through my skull.

I knew this wasn't the end but the beginning.

Jersey

Len and I went to high school together and ran in the same skateboarding and drunken house party circles. He was one grade below me, and that truly mattered back then. Things between us were really fucked up.

It was not hard to figure out that this had a lot to do with my shit childhood and adolescence. My mother went into parenting retirement after the divorce. My father checked the fuck out and married a woman that often made me feel like a giant pile of shit. I latched onto Len like a hungry baby, and when he pulled away because I became too needy, I would scream and rant. After we weren't together, at least not on the books, I would throw myself at anyone who paid me even the least bit of attention.

The first time Len and I hooked up was New Year's Eve in 1990. We were raw ass suburban Jersey teenagers, transitioning into some semblance of adulthood.

I was at a large and unsupervised house in a wealthy housing development, the kind where people drive imported cars and order an endless stream of clothing from the L.L.Bean catalog. Not where I grew up. Not even close. The thing about our high school was that three separate towns spilled into one school, which created a socioeconomic shit show. The wealthier kids came from one town, the working-class kids came from another, and then there was my town: which was known to be trashy. It wasn't to say everyone in my town was trashy, but that was the overarching reputation, especially when I had to tell a mom from the rich town where I lived. It was like a sad eighties movie come to life at our high school.

We were sitting in a sunken living room with oversized and overstuffed couches, waiting for the ball to drop not even a half hour away in Manhattan. Len and I had hung out a bunch of times before. We had friends in common–the skaters and the kids who always hung around in art class. He was tall, and I was short, so I didn't think he liked me, but he did. He put his arm around me on the couch, and I sat there frozen for a while, watching the Times Square debauchery and drinking a Coors Light. He leaned in and said we haven't kissed yet, and then we kissed for a long time. It was the kind of kissing where the skin on my face was rubbed raw.

We were together for about four years, even though at least three and a half of those years were made up of one endless late-night phone fight.

I didn't tell him that I had moved to Milltown. I didn't tell him that I had quit my job at Bennigan's and was now working at Milltown Tavern. We had stopped calling each other maybe six months prior; I was in a detoxification process and didn't want to relapse. I knew that he was going to art school in the city. He lived in an apartment with other art school people in the East Village.

When I would lurk around the city by myself, taking photos with my manual camera and drinking deli coffee, I would imagine running into him. My plan was that I would act all surprised. We'd casually catch up like old friends, maybe sneak a fuck in at his apartment, and not talk for a long time. I wouldn't consider it a relapse because we weren't even talking anymore. But what I totally spaced was that one of my raver roommates was friends with his friend's little sister, and he came into Milltown Tavern one night because he had heard that I was working there.

It was no longer summer by that point. I had been at Milltown Tavern for a few months, still taking temporary refuge in that dumpy raver apartment. But there was talk of an open room coming up in a brownstone where some of the Milltown Tavern peeps lived, so I was mentally able to cope with the subpar conditions for the time being.

I noted a sharp chill in the air when I walked out the door to head to work. I had been practicing my pre-shift ritual to steady myself for the long night ahead. It was a weekend night, and I knew that the show was sold out, which meant it would be busy as fuck. So, I did some yoga, burned jasmine incense, and listened to an Enya CD. I picked out some cute shit to wear and put on black eyeliner, bright blue eyeshadow, and deep red lipstick. It was dark out and was probably close to six on my walk to work.

I put my coat and bag in a cabinet behind the bar and wrote up a ticket for a veggie burger shift meal. It was warm inside, and the large rows of windows, which surrounded Milltown Tavern on two sides, were fogged, creating a womblike atmosphere. I sat in the middle of the dining room and ate alone at a four top. It was starting to get busy, which meant that people who came from out of town were starting to surface for the show. I poured myself a ginger ale and bitters and sat on the floor in the back of the band room. I smoked during sound check before going into the basement to punch in. The band playing that night was called Superchunk. They came in from North Carolina.

While I was downstairs in the office, I could hear a few of the servers chatting and getting high. There was always a packed bowl in the walk-in fridge, complements of the chef. When the huge metal door opened, a cool stinky breeze and three dark haired guys tumbled out as if they were high as fuck pirates walking off a docked boat.

A few moments later, I was behind the bar, rooting around for a clean rag to put in my back pocket when I saw the Len walk in with two people I didn't know. My body shivered all over and not in a good way; it was as if I had been electrocuted.

He was with one guy and one girl, and I figured they were from his art school in the city because they looked NYC-cool and not Jersey-infected. Len wore a big, wool

Guatemalan sweater, baggy Levi jeans, and black Converse. His friends wore all black, were very manicured, and seemed uptight. They sat at a table in the middle of the dining room. I pretended I didn't see them even though I knew Len already saw me. I hid in the band room for a while and smoked again because they wouldn't be allowed in there before the show.

Pete was the other bartender, and his younger brother Mark was the bar back, which meant he had to do whatever we asked him. Pete and I definitely took advantage of our hierarchy.

Kate was also working that night. She was a veteran waitress and part-time manager with a big hive of dirty blond hair that often held together with a chopstick or a pencil. She was born and raised Milltown like Rob. They had grown up together, and it was clear from the start that they secretly hated each other. She was in a semi-famous punk rock band in the eighties and was now married with a kid. A lot of the younger crew called her Mama Kate, because Rob was the mean dad, and the kids needed somewhere to nuzzle in for comfort after we got yelled at.

Vera and Astrid, the two best friends, waited tables and liked to start shit with everyone. Rafa was probably seating people. He was a beautiful human being in his early twenties with bright blue eyes and curly black hair, who may or may not have been Rob's lover.

Besides the kitchen staff, there was Rob. On a busy weekend night, Rob would vacillate between the basement office, the back room, and the pub. He would lean at the end of the bar armed with a pack of King Kools and a Stella Artois. He smoked, drank, and chatted with people. He always knew everything that was going on around him. If I fucked up and let the tap spill over on a Guinness because I was trying to multitask, he would snap at me to get my shit together. I wanted Rob around because I craved praise, but I didn't want him around because then I was afraid that I'd get in trouble. Rob had his favorites. Sometimes I was his favorite, and then sometimes I suddenly lost that privilege even though I didn't know why.

While I was hiding out from Len and the NYC-cool kids, Rob waltzed into the band room and stood by the door while guys set up their post. He looked around the room and walked out. Mark and I were standing in the back, passing a smoke back and forth. We knew we had better get back behind the front bar. The garage doors were open to the street because the roadies were still loading in equipment, and a cold breeze blew in off of the river. I shivered, and Mark put his arm around me. The best part about that band room was that it was generally too loud for conversation, so I could just stand next to someone and be there with them but also could stay in my own head.

When I walked out through the swinging doors, Len stood in the hallway, waiting for the bathroom.

"Hey," I said as casual as possible.

"What are you doing here?" he asked.

"I work here now. I live here too. What are *you* doing here?" I wrapped myself around him. His shape was familiar. His sweater smelled like an animal. "Wait. Why are you here?" I asked him, pulling away.

"We came to see Superchunk."

"Oh, right. You like them," I said.

I had thought about Len when I saw that Superchunk would be playing. I figured he might come to the show. I would think about him every day.

* * *

We got back to my apartment around three in the morning after I closed the bar and after Len went to a diner with his friends. He got into my bed in his jeans and T-shirt. He had taken off the big wool sweater, folded it neatly, and put it on the floor. I pictured rats nesting in the sweater and laughed a little to myself, because I had been trapped in the bathroom with a rat the week prior.

The most unfortunate part of the incident with the rat in the bathroom is that I had consumed half of a hash brownie that one of my roommates had made for an upcoming rave. It was in the bathroom that the deep paranoia struck. Because of the rat situation, I ended up standing on the toilet for at least fifteen minutes until I had the courage to get the fuck out of there.

"What are you laughing at?" he asked.

"There was a rat in the bathroom last week. I was in there with it."

"No, you weren't," he said.

Len never believed me because I lied to him a lot, and he would always find shit out. He would do that thing where he wouldn't have sex with me; we would do everything but fuck, and then the whole next day, I would be rubbed raw and sad. We touched each other a lot and slept maybe an hour. I didn't know how to feel being with Len again. I wanted him, but I also didn't want him, because I knew it was wrong.

"If I hook up with Len again, will you shoot me?" I asked my good friend, Chris, not even a week ago.

"I've shot you many times already, Ana."

When I walked Len out of my apartment the next day, the air was sharp with an autumn chill, and the sun was oppressively bright. It hurt to be outside, to be sleep-deprived and sore from fucking around with someone who wasn't good for me. All I wanted was to crawl back into my dark basement room, even though it was hardly a cocoon.

I could feel Len judging me like he had always judged me because I didn't live in the nicer part town with the wide stoops and the old trees. I lived in the shit part of town with the chicken bones on the sidewalk and the burned-out cars. I could tell that he thought he was better than me now that he was going to a fancy art school and living in the city while I was living in squalor and going to a Jersey state school.

There I was again: that kid from the trashy town, continuously covered in a thick layer of single mom poverty shame.

"I'm moving in a few weeks," I said.

"Oh yeah?"

"To this really nice brownstone."

"That's cool."

I knew he didn't believe me, and I was practically lying anyhow. We hugged at the corner. I knew we wouldn't see each other for a while. Something had shifted; I didn't feel that old obsession. Maybe it was because I had a new job in a new town, and I was meeting all kinds of interesting, smart people.

I went back inside and got back in bed until I had to get ready for work. I'd do it all over again: the yoga, the incense, the Enya, the cute clothes, and the makeup.

Four

Portland

I couldn't work with Drew anymore. Paul had called Josh and told him the shit that had gone down with me and Drew. He said that it was really unprofessional of Drew, that I was his employee and a married woman, and that they should really watch their reputation. I was super fucking embarrassed more than anything.

After working there for a few months, it became pretty damn evident that Josh was the partner who held the studio together. He was responsible for the business end of things; he made sure the clients were happy, the bills were covered, and the employees got paid on time. Drew was the more creative, whimsical partner.

Once I realized this, I became pretty nervous around Josh; I had wanted to please him by doing a good job, and I did. It reminded me a lot of how it was at Milltown Tavern with Rob. I felt like I always needed to please. Josh even told Drew that I was very talented and that maybe they should give me a raise in order to keep me happy.

It was fine because I wasn't sure if I could work with Drew anyhow. I had been sitting on my resignation letter, and I was flipping out about money. If Paul did end leaving me and if I didn't have a job, I would be crazy broke in a city where I hardly knew anyone. We had finally started to settle in after the move; we were able to pay our shit on time and had enough money to get by until the next paycheck. Thinking about being in Portland without any legit support or income, definitely rustled up some old fears about my mom not being able to pay the electric bill and then the lights wouldn't turn on.

Things between Paul and I had made a serious downturn after that night with Drew. In the weeks afterwards, we would either fight, or we would latch onto each other out of fear. There was nothing in between; nothing resembled normal in our lives anymore. When I was on a high and feeling like we could get through it and sleeping with Paul again, he would go into an angry spiral of hatred about me. It made my relationship with Len seem high functioning.

I thought a lot about Len in those manic days. I wanted to be done with the crazy, but now the crazy was back to haunt me.

One evening, Paul and I were home after work. The previous few days had been relatively calm. But out of nowhere, he blurted out that he had called Josh and ratted. It felt like the floor underneath my feet was ripped away, and I didn't know what to do with myself.

"Why did you do that, Paul?" I asked him. "Why the fuck did you tell Josh about what happened with me and Drew?"

"I don't know, Ana. Why did you fool around with Drew?"

"I get it was the wrong thing to do, but that is where I work. This is the most fucked up…" I screamed and cried.

"You should have thought about that when you decided to fuck around with your boss."

There wasn't anything more I could say. He had every right for doing what he did by making that call, but he was kind of wrong for meddling. Josh was Drew's business partner and not his spouse. I had to face this shit the next day at work.

I hardly knew Josh personally. What I did know was that he was a workaholic and his business meant everything to him. Even though things between Drew and I had become awkward in the weeks after our kissing episode, we were still able to work together, and we were able to keep our professional appearances. I managed shit in the office tight and was always respectful.

Drew and I had even stopped going out for lunch and coffee. We had stopped being friends. We became work colleagues.

I went into work the next day after zero sleep. Josh came right up to me at my desk and said we needed talk. When Drew got in, we needed to have a meeting in the back room. I wanted to build a nest under my desk and not come out. I unearthed my resignation letter, did a few minor edits, and printed it out. If I wasn't fired, I would resign. I knew that I fucked up, and that Drew's role was way more important than mine in the end.

When Drew sauntered in some time after ten, Josh walked up and chatted with him quietly by the front door. They retreated into the back room for quite a while. I pretended to write important emails, anticipating their next move. Then Drew came up to me and said that I needed to go into the back room. He looked flustered and upset. A couple of the designers turned around in their swivel chairs. I felt like I had to pee, but I didn't.

I went to the back room and sat at down at the makeshift table. It all happened too fast. Josh was firm in a mean dad kind of way and said that Portland was way too small of a city to have people knowing that there was fraternizing going on at Blatant. He couldn't have these kinds of things jeopardizing their client relationships. He said that it was too close to home since Paul worked in the same business and was clearly angry. He and Drew decided that it was best that I finish out the week. They'd give me two weeks of severance pay, and I could keep my health insurance until the end of the month. I said okay, thanks, and sorry. I felt numb.

"I'm really sorry about this," Drew said when we got back to our desks.

"Me too," I said. "Paul is broken up. He can be really impulsive."

"You'll find something else."

"Yeah," I said. Tears started to well even though I held them back as long as I could.

* * *

On my last day of work, a couple of the designers took me out for lunch, but Drew and Josh didn't join. They said they had a client conference call, which I knew was bullshit. I packed up the few personal things I had on my desk, said a half-assed goodbye, and walked down the dusty stairs for the last time. I felt a sense of relief like when something hard was over, but then it hit me that harder things were to come.

I wasn't sure if my marriage would survive. I wasn't sure if I could survive on my own. I didn't know what I would find when I got home: chill, open-minded Paul or harsh, angry Paul. So, I went straight over to Jess and Dana's.

"What's gonna happen now, Ana?" Dana asked me.

We were sitting at the dining room table. I knew she was asking not only what would happen between me and Paul but what would happen for her and Jess.

"I dunno," I said.

"You think you'll go back to Jersey?"

"Do you think you'll go back to Jersey?"

"Yeah. Maybe. Probably."

We all knew that this was the beginning of the end. We had a short blip of time when there was so much hopefulness. I remembered Jess driving the four of us over a bunch of Portland bridges one night, from east to west and from west to east. We rolled down all the windows even though there was a light chill to the air, and we blasted music, smoked, and laughed.

We didn't know what was ahead of us. It didn't matter, because how bad could it be?

* * *

After I was "let go" from the studio, I had my days free to beat the shit out of myself and to look for a new job. At least Jess and Dana were around during those days. It rained tons, and we were pretty depressed. Jess had been living in Portland for over a year and said it got like that in the winter. Everyone got depressed because it was dark and rainy all the time. She said once spring hit, we wouldn't be depressed anymore. I believed her because I had nothing else to lean on.

The three of us went to a soaking pool, which was in a hotel that used to be an elementary school. There was nothing like that in Jersey. I walked into an old brick schoolhouse and paid a few bucks at the front desk to get access to this beautiful, warm pool. It sat ensconced in a jungle of overgrown Northwest native plants, and it felt like I was somewhere truly magical.

Dana and I changed into our bathing suits in private stalls, but Jess stripped down in the communal locker area. She didn't give a shit. We rinsed off in the outdoor shower before wading into the warmth. The only other person in the pool was this mom in a vintage one piece and her toddler. We went toward the back of the pool, away from the mom and her kid. The three of us sat back with our heads against the tiles, our eyes closed, and it was quiet. It felt good to be outside and to rest in warm water.

In recent weeks, Dana had been talking nonstop about leaving Portland and going back to Jersey because she still couldn't find work. It in turn made Jess upset because she didn't want Dana to leave her alone in the house. And of course, I was all fucked up because I had pretty much ruined my life.

“Why did you marry Paul anyway?” Jess asked, catching me off guard.

“I guess maybe because a lot of my friends from high school were getting married.”

“Yeah, but why would that matter?” Dana asked.

“Maybe I wanted to be normal for once,” I said.

I told them about our wedding. How my friends from high school and a few friends from Milltown Tavern came. Even Rob came with Rafa. A couple of people I knew from college came. Paul’s friends from Brooklyn and a few of his high school friends came. Then there were our families who were both thick old school broods: mine all Italian and his mostly Irish. I told them about how both the ceremony and the reception was at this crazy old, historical Chinese restaurant in a sketchy part of Jersey near Milltown. It upset our traditional families. I wore red instead of white, and Paul wore a vintage suit with no tie. I told them that Paul made a mixed CD for our music.

I remembered the look on some of my family members’ faces when they kissed me goodbye that night. They handed me envelopes of cash, telling me congratulations, but it didn’t feel honest.

I always felt like a disappointment, especially when I was just being myself.

I felt super sad there in the pool. My eyes welled up because I knew my family would be disappointed in me yet again. I had continued to keep what was happening between Paul and I quiet, but soon enough, I would have to tell them everything.

Jess was out of the pool, stretching like a cat. Steam came off her body. The mom and kid went into the locker room, so it was just the three of us in the heavily landscaped pool area. We could hear the kid screaming inside, probably not wanting to get changed. It made me want to scream too. I wished I could scream. I wished I could be a kid again, so I could start everything over and not turn out so fucked up.

"It's like you wanted to be normal to make your family happy, but then you had this totally not normal wedding," Dana said.

"You were invited, you know?"

"I wasn't in a good place," Dana said.

"It's okay."

We were quiet again. A light spring drizzle fell, and it felt good to take in the warmth of the water but to be cooled off by the benign rain. I felt relatively calm for the first time in days. I hadn't been sleeping well and wasn't eating much.

Every evening, Paul would come home from work, and we would get into these intense discussions that left both of us exhausted and in tears with no resolution. We would sleep with our backs facing each other, and he would leave super early in the morning. I would be left alone with my self-loathing for the rest of the day.

The hardest part was that I couldn't call any of my good friends or my family. I wasn't even close to being able to explain what was going on. I couldn't think of one person who would be able to listen unconditionally. My mother would worry like crazy, and my father would be angry and disappointed. I could call my brother, but there was always the risk of him telling the rest of our family. I continually cycled through which friend I could call and just couldn't come up with a true confidant.

Jess and Dana were constantly in financial survival mode, and they became more like company and not necessarily emotional supporters. Paul was in his own existential crisis that involved my actions; I couldn't lean on him. His emotions were all over the place. He kept talking about how he wished his dad was still around. His dad would have been able to give us the right kind of advice. His mom was way too emotional, but his dad would be able to see the whole picture. He kept acting like if his dad wasn't dead, we would be okay. It broke my heart more than anything.

“I gotta get out. My fingers are all wrinkly,” I said to Jess and Dana.

I sat on the side of the pool and stared at my mangled hands. It reminded me of being a little kid. My mom would sit on the toilet when I took a bath, back when I still trusted her. She would tell me it was time to get out when my fingers got wrinkly.

I thought about how my mom would feel when I told her what happened. She adored Paul. Everyone in my family adored him. I knew they felt that they didn’t have to worry about me anymore. My father would be angry with me for messing things up with Paul. I knew that even though he would never admit it, he felt responsible for my shitty childhood. Now that I was married, I was Paul’s charge, so my father was off the hook. He didn’t have to feel guilty because I ended up with a solid person.

I remembered a day not long before Paul and I were due to leave for Oregon. I had driven out to my dad and stepmother’s in the suburbs to have lunch. Things between me and my stepmother had softened a bit since I finished college. It wasn’t that she was that nice to me; it was that I didn’t need to rely on my father as much anymore. So, the threat was lifted. I was on my own, and she could no longer complain about all the shit I did wrong. She continued to have tantrums, but they didn’t involve me personally. I just stayed out of her way.

"You and your mother used to be very close," my father had said that afternoon. We were sitting on the back patio. He had grilled some chicken, and my stepmother had made a salad.

"Really?"

"Absolutely. You two were joined at the hip. I used to carry you around the neighborhood on my shoulders," he said.

My stepmother had left to take the dog out, so he clearly felt free to talk openly about things that he would never talk about around her. It seemed like this was his way of saying that everything was okay for me now. He was referring to the blip of time when my parents were still together, a time that I couldn't remember much because I was too young. I did remember my mother giving me baths and feeling safe, and I did remember my father carrying me around on his shoulders and being happy.

But then I remembered my mother losing her fucking mind, and my father not being around anymore because he was with this new person who demanded everything from him. I never felt safe after that, and I hardly felt happy anymore.

"And now you have Paul," my father said.

"Well, yeah. We have each other," I said.

* * *

In the damp changing area adjacent to the soaking pool, I changed into dry clothes and said goodbye to Jess and Dana. They didn't look like they were going anywhere anytime soon. On the walk home through the chilly drizzles, my head was fogged from the long, hot soak. My body felt warm and limber. I took a thin joint out of my jacket, looked around to make sure nobody could see me, lit it, and took a few drags.

I had started smoking a lot more weed. It was the only thing that could take away the sting of the bad feelings I had for myself. I wandered around the leafy neighborhood, and when I reached a familiar park, I realized that I was only a few blocks from Drew's house. I hadn't been back there since that ill-fated, drunken night. I felt pretty high, and my heart was racing.

I couldn't stop thinking about Drew's messy blond hair falling into his face after we kissed that night. He had this shocked look in his eyes. His blue eyes were not Paul's brown ones. His body was this new shape. There was so much I didn't know about him.

I wanted to know what it was like to grow up in Southern California. What he ate for dinner as a kid. What his room was like, what his schools were like, who his friends were, and who he has had sex with.

And I wanted him to know all of this about me.

I sat under a big tree in the park because it began raining hard. I thought about how I knew Paul so well. It wasn't because we were married. It was because Paul was from where I was from, and that's how we knew each other. It was the familiarity of everything we had ever known. That was also why I loved him and why he loved me, but now I knew that there were different kinds of love, because what I was feeling for Drew was something that I had never felt for Paul.

"Hey. It's Ana. I was gonna leave a message, but..."

"Oh, hey. The heat isn't working at the studio. I'm at home."

"I'm under a tree at that park near your house. Should I stop by?"

"Um. Yeah. Sure," he said.

When the rain let up, I walked the few blocks over to Drew's. During those days, it seemed that my whole entire life happened in that Northeast neighborhood—all within a twenty-block radius. It was like living in Milltown and not needing to venture into the city or the suburbs. I passed sweet little houses with overgrown yards and cats in the windows.

I wished I could trade places with the people who lived there. I wished I were settled enough to be able to live in a house with a yard and a cat, because it seemed as if someone had to be settled to have all those things. There was a middle-aged woman with curly brown hair sitting on a couch on one of the porches, drinking a steamy beverage out of a thick ceramic mug, smoking, and reading the newspaper.

I wanted to be that person. She probably had a normal life. I was sure she was happy.

When I got closer to Drew's, I started running down the street like there was this energy that needed to be released. I remembered feeling like that a lot as a fucked up and frustrated kid. I got a few houses away and slowed down, but then I felt disoriented. Maybe I was on the wrong street. I didn't recognize anything around me.

I sat on a rock wall in front of a house for a minute. My hair was still wet from the pool and the rain, and my face was on fire. This was a literal crossroad in my life, and I could feel it deep in my body. I could have walked home and called a friend. I could've allowed myself to be vulnerable, confided to someone about my fucked-up situation, and take whatever advice they wanted to give me. I could have called my brother and risked the rest of my family finding out that I had cheated on Paul. But I didn't do any of those things.

Drew answered the door in a bright yellow T-shirt with black graphics, jeans, and glasses. I had never seen Drew in glasses. His hair was pulled back into a rubber band, and he seemed like a different person. We sat together on the couch. I took off my shoes and pulled my legs closer to my body. There was a layer of silence between us. We had a lot to say, but it was obvious that neither of us had any words.

"Why is your hair wet?" he asked.

"It's raining," I said.

I didn't want Drew to know that I had been with Jess and Dana at the soaking pool. He knew Jess still spoke with Paul, and of course there was that awkward thing where I tried to set him up with her. I fell into his chest. He could have chosen to not move. I would have gotten the message. But he put his arms around my waist and put his face near my neck.

"You smell like you were in a pool," he said.

"That's weird."

He pulled me close and kissed me. I looked up at him, and it felt as if he was glowing, a heat radiating through our bodies. It felt like a dream, but it wasn't. It became endless hours of exploring and investigating unfamiliar body shapes.

I knew I had to end things with Paul. I loved him too much, and even though I loved him in a fundamentally different way than I might someday love Drew, I couldn't manage the up and down of our relationship any longer. I had developed strong feelings for someone else, and even though I tried to shove those feelings away, I couldn't any longer. I was ashamed of my mistakes, the sloppiness of my emotions, and the ability that I had to hurt someone who I loved. But, as I would tell people in the years following my break from Paul, there was nothing I could do but move away from Paul and toward Drew.

The rawness and intense charge of the feelings I had for Drew had already taken over.

Jersey

The day I moved out of my first apartment in Milltown, the raver roommates scowled at me through their glitter-encrusted eyes. I was in the kitchen packing up a few things when they both walked past me without saying anything. I knew they felt judged because I was leaving, and they were staying as if I was abandoning them. Like the apartment wasn't good enough for me, but it would have to be okay for them. It was as if I had moved up a socioeconomic step by moving a few blocks away to a crumbling down brownstone.

I did kind of judge them though because they were strung out on ecstasy every fucking weekend and wore big-ass pants with dirty ripped cuffs.

And there was the time one of them broke down my door because she thought I had borrowed a pair of her pants without asking. A brick of ramen was missing from the kitchen once, and one of them thought it was me who took it. Another time, I was trying to sleep and asked if they could tone down the techno beats, but my request just escalated the tension that had been building since I moved in. I was just trying to build some semblance of a decent life for myself that didn't involve rats, an endless supply of oversized clothes, and bad techno music.

My friend Mark from Milltown Tavern came over to help me move. We rolled up my futon mattress and secured it with electrical tape for easy transport. The two of us walked through Milltown like a couple of hobos with sticks, laughing and dropping the dumb futon on the dirty sidewalk the whole way over to the new place. There was still a nip in the air, but we were sweating like crazy. We unrolled the futon out in the brownstone's dining room, went back, and carried a few boxes of books and some black garbage bags of clothes down the block.

For the rest of the day, we sat on the floor, smoking and going through my books. We compared what we've both read. Mark noticed that I had a stack of well-worn journals.

"Do you write?" he asked.

"Sometimes. But mostly just really bad poetry. I've been working on a story though about a young guy who sells his jeans for beer instead of looking for a job. It's called *Generation L*...for loser."

"That's pretty funny," he said. "I'd love to read it when you're done."

"Oh man. I dunno," I said.

We listened to Björk's *Post* on CD and drank a few beers. Afterward, Mark left to go read downstairs, and I unpacked more of my shit and wandered around the apartment.

Even though there was a lot of crumbling plaster and splintering hardwoods, it was a beautiful, old, and comforting house. It was the second floor flat in a three-story brownstone that was owned by a retired Filipino doctor. There was a guy who would come around from time to time to sweep the stoop or mess with the plumbing, but other than that, "the doctor," as we called him, didn't do much in terms of repair. He left us alone and didn't charge super high rent, so we left him alone too. That was the silent agreement.

There had been a rotating cast of Milltown Tavern characters that had moved in and out of the brownstone since the early eighties. When I moved in, I got the dining room, which was pretty much this big open space that was sectioned off with a screen that a former roommate had left behind.

Julio, who was an on and off Milltown Tavern server, had the big bedroom upstairs, and his sometimes girlfriend Michelle was there. If they were in a fight, she wasn't around, which was most of the time. In the smaller bedroom upstairs was Rene, a prep cook who was originally from Venezuela. Downstairs in the first-floor apartment was Mark's brother Pete and his girlfriend Mel. Like Julio's girl, Mel was also hardly around, but it was not because they fought a lot. She worked an office job and spent a lot of time at her parents' place in the city.

Mark basically lived on the floor in Pete's kitchen. He stashed a few blankets in the hall closet, and when he wanted to get some sleep, which seemed to be pretty rare, he took out his bedroll and slept on the kitchen floor.

All the way downstairs in the small basement apartment was an older couple who were somehow related to the landlord. They had been living down there for many years. The aromas from their cooking wafted through the entire house and made me dry heave most mornings. But they were kind people, nonetheless.

It took a few weeks, but I settled into my digs and had even bought a frame for the futon mattress. I was finally feeling like a real person.

But then my father came into Milltown. My car wasn't working right, and the idea was that he was going to follow me to the mechanic he always used in case I broke down on the way there. I couldn't afford to fix my own car. I had to get to my classes during the weekdays, so my dad still helped me with those things on the sly, without telling my stepmother.

It was in the middle of the afternoon, and my father pulled up and double-parked in front of the brownstone. A lot of people double-parked in Milltown; it was part of the cultural landscape. I came out to greet him. He was standing on the stoop, looking up at the building. It was certainly in a state of disrepair, but nothing like the last place I had lived in, which I knew better than to ever expose him to.

"These steps need to be fixed," he said, picking a weed out of the cracked concrete and throwing it onto the sidewalk.

"They won't do those things. It's what keeps the rent down," I said.

It was clear that he wasn't interested in coming inside, and I didn't want him to anyhow. If he had, he would have seen an okay place. There was probably a pile of dishes in the sink, but other than that, the bones of the place were charming, and the floors were shiny. My father was raised in Brooklyn during the great depression. He had lived in a lot of cold-water flats because his father had struggled to make ends meet. They would move to dodge rent. I had a feeling that thus brownstone reminded him of that time.

I couldn't shake the scrutiny vibes for the rest of the day. I felt a lot of pride in moving out of the rave-den-of-techno-dread and into the crumbly hipster brownstone. I drove down Route 3 West with my father trailing behind me, doing what I could to tuck my feelings away and to not worry about breaking down on the highway. I blasted New Order's *Substance* on the tape deck, passing the strip malls, the diners, and the car lots—the soundtrack and the landscape of my early twenties.

I couldn't imagine being anywhere else.

Luckily, I made it to my dad's mechanic without breaking down. We dropped my car off and headed straight back into Milltown, about twenty minutes away. We listened to the jazz on the radio and didn't talk about much. He would talk about the past but only the good memories and not the bad ones. He wouldn't talk much about what was really true in the present, like what I was up to in life. He would ask me how school was going, and I would often give him a canned answer.

"It's good," I would say. But I wasn't doing well in school. I skipped classes a lot and couldn't stay focused. I was tired from working late and sleeping odd hours, and college just wasn't a priority. I should have dropped out and taken a break, but I stayed in school and half-assed it most of the time.

When we got to Milltown, we drove slowly through town.

"You know, I used to take you here when you were a kid. We'd eat at that old Italian restaurant. I think it's still around."

"Oh yeah. I remember that. It's still there," I said.

"It reminds me of Brooklyn here."

"Yeah, me too. That's why I like it here," I said.

When we pulled up to the brownstone, I kissed my father on the cheek, got out of the car, and ran up the stoop. I wanted to disappear. I didn't want to think about my dad taking me on those little dates when I was a kid, because that was before he met my stepmother. I didn't want to think about her. I didn't want to think about how my father was disappointed in me because I lived in a rundown brownstone. I realized he was concerned for me; I had lived in a shit apartment with my mother, and he didn't want that for me again. He just didn't know how to tell me those things.

* * *

I dated an undercover cop for a minute and lost my fucking head over him.

He was one of my roommates' friend's cousin. He came into Milltown Tavern one night to see Built to Spill. I knew he was a cop; he copped drugs for a living. He would go into work dressed up like a junkie. He rented a room from an elderly Polish woman in the East Village. That's all I knew about him, but I wanted to know more.

It had been a few months since I saw Len, the now true ex, but I was still fucked up over him. It wasn't that I still pined for him, but I was afraid that nobody would ever yearn for me. When I would go into the city, I would still create stories about running into him. I would make a point of walking down University Place, so I could pass by his art school.

When the cop came into Milltown Tavern, I was sidled up behind the bar next to Mark. He was putting bottles of beer into the cooler, and we were smoking and laughing about dumb shit. Rob was downstairs in the office, so we were doing busy work while fucking around in case he came up. I cut lemons and limes and filled the plastic fruit trays. I looked up and saw the cop, and my heart skipped.

"Hey," Shawn said to Mark and me.

"Hey, man. How's it going?" Mark said, shaking Shawn's hand and acting all formal like guys do sometimes.

"Hey," I said.

"Cool. Can I have a Rolling Rock?"

I opened a beer and put it on the bar under a napkin. He gave me a five, and I walked to the register to ring him up. I wanted to stay there, but I brought back his change instead. He chatted with Mark a little bit about the band. I was too nervous in my stomach to engage in their conversation, feeling like I would never have anything to add, like I was a child. When Mark walked off to change the keg in the basement, I was left alone with Shawn.

“I like your haircut. You look different,” Shawn said, smiling.

“Oh, thanks,” I said and looked down at the spilling over tray of fruit.

I recently had my shoulder length hair cut into a pixie. I bought a bunch of new clothes. I was making decent money, and I felt strong and secure for the first time in my life. Shawn smiled again, grabbed his beer, and went to sit at a table with his cousin and a few friends who had come in from the city. He wore spongy creeper shoes and a short sleeve button down. He also had his super dark hair greased back. I liked it. I never knew anyone who looked like that.

“That guy likes you. But he’s a fucking cop,” Mark whispered in my ear.

“Shut the fuck up,” I said, punching Mark in the arm. We both started laughing super hard, falling over, and punching each other even more.

During the show, the front room was practically empty. Pete was working the bar with me, but he was mostly drinking Guinness out of a coffee cup and going in and out of the back room to smoke and watch the band. All the dudes at work seemed to be nuts about Built to Spill. As much as I’d like to say that I knew their music and could bond with them, I didn’t. I went back there a few times to smoke, and even though the music was pretty vibrant and electric, I was way more interested in pining over Shawn. He stood in the back next to his cousin and those friends from the city. I looked over, caught his eye, waved, and stood by the door, bopping my head like I was engrossed in the music.

When I went back out front, it was calm and quiet. I sat on the cooler and couldn't stop thinking about how Shawn liked my haircut. I kept looking at Rob, who was sitting at a café table with two highly manicured women and a guy in all black. Probably important music industry people.

A cluster of people walked in and stood at the door. Rafa should have been seating people, but he was sitting with Rob and the music people. Of course, Rob never gave Rafa shit for fucking around on the job; he got different treatment. There were people who Rob gave shit to, and there were people who Rob let do whatever the fuck they wanted. That hierarchy was constantly shifting but never for Rafa.

"Where are all the servers?" I asked Pete.

"Who fucking knows. In the back maybe. Or downstairs."

Kate was watching the band, and everyone else was probably downstairs getting high. Rob gave me a look and turned his head toward the people waiting by the door. I went over to them, grabbed a few menus, and seated them at a table in the middle of the room. Astrid came up from downstairs and went over to take their order. After a minute or two, she came up to the middle of the bar where the servers brought their drink orders. She put down the ticket, and I poured her three pints and a Jim Beam on the rocks.

"Thanks, little Ana," she said, blowing me a kiss with those huge red lips. "Oh and tell those yuppie assholes that they can eat my pussy," she said, referring to the new table she was waiting on: three guys in baseball hats.

Nobody at Milltown Tavern could stand the guys in the baseball hats who worked investment jobs in the city. They had asked Astrid if we had a TV, so they could watch the game. That put her over the edge. She and Vera had been working at Milltown Tavern for a few years already. They were born and raised Milltown, and because of that, Rob treated them differently. They mostly got to do what they wanted.

When Kate came up from the band room, she went over to Rob's table to see if they needed anything. She took all the music people tables because she was once a music person and wasn't intimidated by them. She was firm, but I knew I could go to her for anything because she knew how everything worked. If I went to Rob, it could turn into an epic tantrum, so I always went to Kate first.

"They want their bill," Kate said. She wrote some things on the ticket before handing it to me and sticking the pen into her beehive.

"Should I comp anything?"

"Just Rob's two beers," she said, laughing and grooving to the rockabilly music that played out front.

I rang up the check and handed it to Kate.

The band room door opened, and all the loud music spilled in. That's when Shawn came back to the bar. I looked up at him and felt many things. He was a striking presence. He had this dark edge; the dyed black hair contrasted with his super light skin and his drastic Boston accent.

"The back bar is packed. Can I get another Rolling Rock?"

"Oh yeah," I said, opening the beer.

"Hey, do you maybe wanna hang out next week?" he asked, catching me off guard.

"Oh. Sure," I said, looking down at the bar. I caught myself and looked back up at him.

"I'm off on Thursday," he said.

"Okay. Cool."

I wrote down my number on a bar napkin. Shawn smiled and went back to the band room. The super loud music spilled into the room again. I didn't have Thursday off, but I could force someone to work for me.

It was hard getting through the rest of the night. I was distracted. I even broke a glass in the sink that we rinsed them in, which was a fucking ordeal because I had to drain the sink and make sure no glass chards were left. I somehow managed to clean it all up without Rob noticing, but my hands were shaking the whole time, afraid of getting caught. Pete just stared at me, standing there smoking and laughing because he knew how riled I was over this cop.

People piled into the front room when the music ended, so Mark, Paul, and I were crazed. We poured pints and shots and opened bottles of beer for the rest of the night. We hardly had time to come up for air. I even forgot about Shawn for ten minutes. I knew he was sitting at a table near the front windows with his friends, and every once in a while, I would look over to see if he was still there. He came over before he left.

"I'll give you a call next week," he said.

"Okay. Sounds good."

For the rest of the night, I didn't hear the end of it from Mark and Pete. They told me I could never bring Shawn around the house, because he's a cop and a narc.

It had been a crazy night as it was with all the sold-out shows, and we were all pretty worn out, ready to have beers, smoke, and shoot the shit by the time everyone left. While Pete and I closed out the registers, and Mark cleaned up all the strewn cups and bottles in the back room, a bunch of the usual suspects hung around the bar after hours, playing music on the jukebox. Pete kept playing songs from Pavement's *Slanted and Enchanted*, and Rob didn't give him shit for once because he was in such a good mood. When Rob was in a good mood, us kids could do no wrong.

Jerry Russo came in to close the bar up. It was hard to explain the role that Jerry played at Milltown Tavern. He was kind of like a manager but also kind of like a babysitter. He was the combination of an older gay man and an Italian grandma. I noticed he turned up when Rob was too drunk, high, or both. He came to make sure the bar was locked up, and that all of the cash was locked away in a safe downstairs.

Jerry lived in the building that Rob owned next door, and I could tell that there was ongoing tension between them that may or may not have something to do with Rafa, who was clearly on the Rob dole. Rafa was supported by Rob, but he sometimes lived at Jerry's apartment.

Jerry took out a bag of pot, cut it up with a tiny cuticle scissors, and proceeded to roll a couple of joints that were soon passed around. Rob and Jerry had grown up together and were like eternally feuding brothers. We were all smoking the joints, drinking Rolling Rocks, and getting pretty buzzed. Astrid, Vera, and Kate danced to Blondie. Out of nowhere, Rob started breaking dishes in the kitchen. I thought it was urban legend that Rob broke dishes because I had heard the lore many times, but clearly it was a real thing. Some of the guys were sucking the nitrous out of whip cream cans and falling down on the ground. A few of the local regulars were still at the bar, groping for beers and laughing at the tomfoolery.

Jerry puttered around the bar, recounting the money and making sure everything was tallied up. He turned off the lights, put the chairs on the tables, wiped down the surfaces, and shook his head. He was the one who told us when it was finally time to go. He cleaned up Rob's broken dishes off the floor and made sure Rob got home okay, even though it all transpired in a silence that was laced in animosity.

As much as I would look back at those nights with fondness and nostalgia, I felt extreme unease in those moments. There was this level of chaos in the air that was hard for me to tolerate. I drank a little, and I got a little high sometimes, but I never got too wasted at work. When things would get out of control at Milltown Tavern, I wanted to run away, but I couldn't. I still needed to pretend that I was a part of it all because if I didn't, Rob would feel judged and would ice me out. I couldn't take that risk.

When it was finally time to leave, which always felt like a fucking eternity on the busy, chaotic nights, Mark, Pete, and I decided to walk home even though it was late. My feet ached, and my back was killing me from standing all night, but I had a pocketful of cash and didn't have to be back at work for a few more days. I knew we would stay up for a few more hours. We walked through a darkened and desolate Milltown, and I felt so many little warm tingles in my body, thinking about Shawn even though I was certain he would never call. He'd lose my number or just blow me off.

* * *

"You're nice to look at," he said to me.

I couldn't move, and I couldn't speak. Shawn leaned toward me and put his mouth to mine. We were in the back of a tiny dark bar in the city, just off West Houston on the Soho side. It was dimply lit by a few small votive candles. We had come from dinner at Jean-Claude: steak frites, milky pasta, and table wine. He knew the owners, and people kept coming over to talk. Now, we were deep into these strong, dark beers.

Shawn and I kissed more and drank more of that fragrant beer. We smoked and touched each other. It was early morning late, and the bar would close soon. He didn't call me until after ten to make plans. I was crawling out of my skin by the time the phone rang, thinking for sure that he wasn't going to call. But I would soon learn that this was how he lived—in the late-night hours.

He drove me home in an unmarked police car through the yellow-lit tunnel back to Jersey. It was the car he used for work when he would dress up and arrest drug dealers in dangerous inner-city neighborhoods. He drove fast. The sky was a deep blue, and the light was muted when we spilled out into Jersey and headed through the smokestacks and the industry toward Milltown. It was hard to find parking, so we circled a bunch of times before finding a spot. By the time we found somewhere to park, people were leaving for work.

My housemates were sleeping and probably wouldn't be up for a while. It was quiet when we got inside. A few garbage trucks were charging through town, and some lights were on in neighboring windows. Shawn took out a small gun and tucked it underneath a couch cushion. We sat on the couch and kissed a lot, touching each other more than at the bar. I kept thinking about the gun underneath us like it could go off and shoot us.

"What kind of gun is that? It's small," I said.

"It's called a snub nose. I carry it cause you never know who might follow me."

"I bet nobody would follow you to Milltown," I said jokingly, but he didn't laugh.

He looked at me with those wide, dark eyes. He already knew I wanted to know more about what he did. "It's called buy and bust," he told me. "I go in and buy the drugs, and when I come out, my partner goes in and arrests the dealer."

Now I was the one with the wide eyes. He told me how he goes into the police station and puts on makeup that makes him look like an addict. Fake track marks. Pale makeup to make him look even paler. Dark circles under his eyes even though his eyes were already dark.

I heard someone get up, flush the toilet upstairs, and shut their bedroom door. We stopped talking. I didn't want to end up fucking. I wanted a few more of those sweet dinners in the city first. I didn't remember if he put it there, but my hand went over his hard cock, and I pulled it away.

"This is too much," I said. I moved away from him on the couch.

"Okay… I should get back to the city."

He seemed disappointed, but after a few moments, he kissed me sweetly on the lips. He buttoned up, tucked his shirt into his jeans, buckled up his belt, and put on his shoes. He stood up, took that gun out from under the couch, and tucked it somewhere deep into his pants.

I walked Shawn downstairs, and we hugged hard on the stoop. He was taller than me, so he kissed me on the top of my head as he held me tight. It was a bright early summer morning, drenched in the sun. People walked their dogs, got into cars, and headed toward the train to the city. I looked at Shawn as he walked away, and I liked everything I saw. We didn't talk about hanging out again. I walked back upstairs and got some money, so I could go get a bagel and a coffee.

I sat on the stoop, thinking about everything that happened with Shawn—the kissing, the touching, and the feelings.

Five

Portland

To say I didn't want to hurt someone I loved but then I ended up doing just that was not only in sad movies. I know because I lived it during many long, cold, wet months of winter. The rain seeped into my bones like a relentless stream of loneliness. I did it to myself. I did it to Paul. I did it to our families. I did it to everything that I had built from the floor up: all the stable parts of my life that I worked hard to establish. They all got torn down and reconstructed into a strange, new reality.

While everything was coming apart, I was also falling desperately in love, a painful kind of love.

A young woman, not yet done with her twenties, lived in a puddle. She cried a lot because she missed the man she was abandoning, her best friend, and she pined for the family and friends from where she grew up. They were all the way across the country, and they didn't know that she was suffering because to let them know would make it all the more real. At least without them knowing, she was able to pretend for a few minutes that she wasn't such a mean loser asshole.

"I wanted to run into Hawthorne Street at lunch so a car would hit me," Paul said to me one evening after he got home from work.

"Wait. What did you just say?"

We were in our apartment. We had been eating together most evenings, still holding onto some semblance of married life. When Paul would go to bed, I would go see Drew. Both Paul and I knew how we were living wasn't right, but we didn't know what else to do. Both of us grasped hard to okayness.

This went on for weeks and months. It went on through the darkness of winter. I would come home and sleep on the futon in our spare room. I never spent the night at Drew's. But sometimes, I would crawl into bed with Paul, and we would hold each other until we fell asleep.

"Are you serious? You wanted to run into the street?" I asked him.

"I felt it, but I knew I wouldn't actually do it."

The panic set in deep. I pictured Paul getting run over by a car. I imagined me getting the call. It felt like I had killed him, which I knew that I kind of did. Paul sat at the kitchen table, messing around with a plate of pasta. He wouldn't talk.

"I need to call your therapist," I said. My hands trembled as I grabbed for the house phone.

"I only just thought about it, Ana. I wouldn't..."

I made him give me the number of the therapist he had been seeing since things started to disintegrate. He relented and part of me felt like he wanted this attention.

We had gone in together to see his therapist for a session the week prior. She wanted to meet me, and I liked her immediately. She was a well-dressed, middle-aged woman with long brown hair who worked out of a light, airy office not far from our apartment. I felt such relief sitting there, as if someone was taking on some of my burdens. She had this mellow, neutral perspective; I didn't feel vindicated even though Paul was her client, and his needs came first.

"Would you be open to sharing her?" the therapist had asked Paul, catching us both off guard.

"What does that even mean?" he asked.

"Being okay with Ana being intimate with both you and this other person."

I sat there, staring at the wall. She had a collection of Buddhist statues and esoteric artwork that made me feel warm inside. She offered us tea in handmade ceramic mugs.

I could totally see continuing to live with Paul, sharing a home and finances, but only being intimate with Drew. Since

I had started seeing Drew, Paul and I had sex a few times, but I really didn't want to be with him that way anymore. I didn't know why I didn't. I didn't know why for a lot of things back then.

"Nah. That's not for me," Paul said.

"I would be open to it," I blurted out, which visibly angered Paul.

"What's going on with you, Paul? What are you feeling?" she asked him

"Oh, just picturing Ana with him. Like her having sex with him."

I looked at the clock and was relieved to see that the session was almost over. This was a conversation that Paul and I hadn't broached. I knew I needed to talk to him about these things, but I didn't want to. The room was quiet and heavy.

"I understand," she said.

She said we were almost out of time and that she wanted to leave a few minutes to unwind before we left since she didn't want the session to end on such a heavy note. She told us that we could come in together again if Paul felt that it was helpful.

But now, the therapist didn't answer her phone, so I left her a message, saying that I was scared about Paul. I said that he talked about running into a busy street.

We tried to eat even though neither of us wanted much to do with food. It seemed like we hardly ate much in those days. When the therapist phoned me back a few minutes later, she remained quiet on the line. She listened to me. My voice was a little shaky, but I was able to give her the facts. She gave me the number of an emergency mental health clinic where I could take him. She did not seem overly concerned. I was used to everyone going into a panic over any little fucking thing in my family.

Paul didn't want to go to the clinic. He kept reiterating that he only *thought* about running into the street and that he would never do it. I believed him.

I knew something about this was tied to his father. I had gone into our bedroom the previous morning while he was at work and found myself staring at a photo of Paul's father holding him as a baby. Even though I had seen that photo many times, I looked at it more closely. I noticed such a striking resemblance between Paul as an adult and his father at the age the photo was taken. Same straight short, dark hair and light green eyes. Same dark plaid button down. Same adoring look.

What would Paul be like as a father? I knew he would be a wonderful, doting father. He would never be the father of my child though. I stood there and wept uncontrollably for a long time.

When he got home that evening, I told Paul that I was taken aback while looking at that photo. He was surprised by how moved I was. It was as if he thought that I had already stopped loving him, that I had already stopped caring about him. I tried to tell him that I still cared and that it was complicated. He told me that his father was around his age at the time the photo was taken.

"I feel like I'm disappointing my dad by what's going on with us," he told me.

"What do you mean?" I asked.

He meant his short-lived marriage was failing. He felt he was just sitting there, letting me go off at night to be with this other person. But I also knew a lot of what was going on between us was drudging up old grief. He lost his dad when he was a teenager and has probably tucked those feelings away like any kid would at that age.

We picked up our dinner plates and went into the kitchen, continuing to remain in the domestic roles that had developed over the past year. I scraped and rinsed while he loaded the dishwasher. I wiped up the table and the counters, and he put things away.

"Do you want to talk more?" I asked him.

He went to the back room and shut the door. I went outside, sat on the grass, and called my brother, Michael.

"I met someone else, and now Paul is freaking out. He talked about running into the street. He's losing it, and I'm all the way out here and don't know what..." I said, choking back tears.

My brother was quiet on the line. It was around eleven at night back in Jersey, and it sounded like he was sleeping when I called. "Ana, you have to slow down. I don't know what you're talking about," he said.

"I've been seeing someone from that place I was working at, and Paul and I are probably breaking up. I don't want anyone in our family but you to know."

I lost it. I sobbed uncontrollably. I told him that I had to call him back. He made me promise that I would call him first thing in the morning.

I went for a walk.

I had left the house without a jacket but kept walking anyhow. It was wet, windy, and cold. I was uncomfortable, but it felt sobering to be away from the apartment, away from Paul. I walked past a wet cedar fence, and the scent was so strong. It reminded me of when Paul and I had first arrived in Portland. If only I could go back to the day when I smelled that cedar fence for the first time, back when I was hopeful about living in this new city and making a new life with Paul.

If only I could make everything from that point on go away. If only I could start all over again.

I didn't go see Drew. I went back home and crawled into bed next to Paul. I slept long and hard that night; it was the best sleep since all of this happened. I woke up after Paul had left for work. I made some coffee and called my brother. I told him everything. As I spoke, I could feel something dark and heavy that had been sitting in my body rise up and release.

We talked about practical things. Whereas our parents would freak the fuck out, my brother had lived through his own messy relationship. He had married pretty young and separated after only a few years.

Michael told me that he would lend me some money for an apartment deposit, but I needed to focus on getting a job. I was relieved and agreed to start looking for work right away, even if I had to lean on waiting tables or bartending again.

"What's this guy like anyhow?" he asked.

"Oh, I dunno. He's mellow. He's different," I said.

"Cool, Ana." There was a long pause. "Listen. As long as you're okay. I just wanna make sure you're okay," he said.

"I'll be fine."

We got off the phone, and I felt sad but also relieved that I had support outside of Jess and Dana. By this point, Jess had been hanging out with Paul a lot more. She had been inviting him over and introducing him to more of her artist friends. Dana was still talking about leaving Portland. She and I hung out a lot and had even been talking about getting a place together if she decided to stay and could actually find work. Maybe I would just use my brother's money and let Dana crash with me for a while.

I poured myself another cup of coffee, made some toast, and sat at the computer to start combing for work. I looked around at Paul's things. His records. His books. His artwork. I wondered if it was too hard for him to stay in the apartment that we shared together. I was too distracted to focus on jobs. I was stuck, looking at all of Paul's things that would soon not be in my life anymore, and then I got stuck on my brother and how concerned he was for me.

I knew it reminded him about when I was a kid. I was constantly shuffled between my mom's shithole apartment and my dad's big house. My brother wanted stability for me, and I knew he thought that I had finally found that in Paul.

It was pissing rain outside, and even though it was daytime, it was dark inside the apartment. This was something that had become harder for me to deal with: not just the constant rain but also the darkness and the grayness. It was hard, but I wanted to embrace it; I wanted to feel all the things that needed to be felt.

This was something Paul never understood about me. I would lean into the darkness. I wanted to feel the heaviness, and I would move into my sadness. I would listen to music and go into my head. It was something I had done when I needed somewhere to go when there was nowhere else to go. It started as far back as listening to R.E.M. in my room at my mom's dingy apartment as an escape from my fucked up adolescent reality.

"I don't like seeing you like this, Ana," Paul had said to me once.

He had just moved in with me in the Milltown brownstone, and we were smoking weed and listening to music. He played a bunch of music: a few old jazz records and some newer music from Chicago. I put on a Jeff Buckley CD and went inside for a while. I sat on a chair, put my head in my hands, and rocked back and forth.

"I just feel like I should do something to make you feel better," he had said to me.

After that, I could never listen to music in that way with Paul around. It freaked him out. He didn't get it. But now I could. So, I lit some candles, sat on the floor, and played Jeff Buckley's *Grace* really fucking loud.

I was able to feel what it would feel like to lose Paul, to lose that sense of stability I had been craving my whole life. I felt what it was like to miss my friends back in Jersey, to not have that unconditional love and acceptance to fall back on. I felt what it felt like to be far away from my family, to not have anywhere to hide anymore. And I felt what it felt like to be alone with nobody to tell me not to feel all those things that needed to be felt.

Jersey

I woke to urban chaos in the late morning: the honking of car horns, the crashing of trash cans, and the blaring of sirens. I washed my face, brushed my teeth, and threw on some clothes. I headed through Milltown to the train station.

When I got into the city, I headed crosstown toward the East Village, clutching a deli coffee. I bought the story collection *Jesus' Son* by Denis Johnson at St. Mark's Bookshop. Mark and Pete were talking about the book the night before. It was after our shift, and we were at the old, greasy spoon diner in Milltown, eating grilled cheese and fries and smoking. They were both well-read liberal arts college dropouts.

"Oh fuck. You've never read that book?" Pete asked me.

"You gotta read it, dude! You'd really like it," Mark said.

"Okay. Okay. I will," I said, nipping a soggy fry off of Mark's plate.

When I got home that night, I could feel an emotional shift inside of me. I felt alive and inspired, like I had finally found somewhere to belong. I had found friends who I could relate to, who had smart things to say, and who actually liked me and respected my thoughts.

It was unusually mellow in the city because it was a Saturday in deep summer. Anyone with money had gone away for the weekend. They were at the beach houses in the Hamptons or down the Jersey shore with sunburns, bad hangovers, and confusion about who was sleeping next to them in a sandy bed. I sat in Tompkin's Square Park and smoked a cigarette, trying to read, but the sun was heating up the concrete, and it smelled like piss. I made my way back to the train, so I could chill out on the brownstone stoop.

Mark heard me come in, so he came up from his downstairs apartment. It was the middle of the day, but he was just waking up. I sat and read while Mark brewed a pot of Café Bustelo on the stove in a large stainless steel espresso maker. The smell of the super strong coffee wafted through the apartment. My roommate, Julio, came down from his room and Pete came up. We all sat around the dining room table, drinking coffee and stealing each other's cigarettes out of the ashtray.

"So, what the fuck ever happened with you and Shawn?" Julio asked me when Mark and Pete went back downstairs.

Julio knew Shawn pretty well. They had hung out a bunch, because he was pretty tight with Shawn's cousin. They worked at a restaurant together.

“I’m not sure. He hasn’t called,” I said, looking down at the table.

Julio smiled. “Yeah, he’s a dark dude. He retreats sometimes.”

I knew he was referring to the kind of work Shawn did. The risks involved. I also knew that Shawn drank a lot in different ways than anyone else in my life drank a lot. What I didn’t say was that I had been torn the fuck up since that night in the city with Shawn. I couldn’t get him out of my head. It was as if the time we had spent together had turned into scenes that were stuck on repeat. I couldn’t stop thinking about the way his mouth felt and the way he tasted when we kissed. His kisses were so soft and kind but deep. I couldn’t stop thinking about the way his skin felt and how it smelled when I put my face into his neck.

I wanted so much more of that; it was a deep craving. Every time the phone rang in my apartment, I jumped. Every time the door opened at Milltown Tavern, I looked over. I woke up every day, thinking it might be the day we would hang out again. But the days passed, and if the phone was for me, it wasn’t Shawn.

* * *

I had just gotten back to Milltown from a few hazy, drunken days at the Jersey shore with some old friends from high school. The whole time, I was at that shoddy rented beach house. Between the beers, the cigarettes, and the hot sand, I would run across the street to use the pay phone to check the house answering machine. I wanted to see if Shawn had left a message, but he didn't.

When I was ready to give up on him, he finally fucking called.

"Is this Ana?" he asked.

"Oh. Yeah. Hey." I knew who it was right away, and my heart went crazy inside. I sat on the floor.

"I'm really sorry it took me this long to call. I've been thinking about you. Something happened at work..." he said, trailing off. His voice cracked.

He told me that on the Fourth of July, in the bad parts of the city, things got really fucking crazy. People went up on rooftops to shoot their guns because the noise got masked by all the fireworks. That day, they could get away with it, and the cops had to be on extra alert. He went in to buy heroin in some building, but something happened to him that he couldn't really talk about. He ended up having to go to the hospital. He said that he has been really fucked up, but he was okay now and wanted to see me again.

I just sat there, on the floor of my apartment with the cordless phone in my lap, in some kind of bizarre dream state. We made plans for the following Sunday evening. He would come over, and we would go out somewhere in Milltown.

I spent the following days in a distracted fog. I lived on cigarettes and coffee. My hands shook when I poured pints of beer at work. Every time the phone would ring at home or at work, or if the red light blinked on the answering machine, I thought it would be Shawn calling to cancel our plans.

"What the fuck is wrong with you, Ana?" Rob asked me one night.

I was staring out the window with a bar rag in my hand, randomly wiping down a table in the dining room when he sidled up beside me. It was a slow night, and no bands were playing, so I was the only one behind the bar.

"Oh, sorry," I said.

Rob walked away and down the stairs to his office, which I knew was a warning sign to pull my shit together.

I didn't want to fuck things up at work. The last thing I needed was to get on Rob's bad side. I had heard a story about another bartender who followed someone in a famous band on tour. The day she got home, the band guy called her at Milltown Tavern and broke up with her. For weeks—months maybe—she came to work in a daze until Rob couldn't take it anymore and fired her mid shift. She left crying and moved to Seattle to stalk that band guy.

I didn't want to go out like that. Milltown Tavern meant too much to me. I would never find another place to work where I made decent money and got to be around people who I actually liked and who liked me.

When Sunday evening came, I waited for Shawn on the stoop. I was a little tan and wore this flowery hippie halter top that I had bought at a shop on Long Beach Island. I smoked and pretended to read *Jesus' Son*, peering up every few minutes when a car would come down my block. I hardly slept the night before, thinking he would bail.

"I saw you look up from your book," he said when he walked up to the brownstone.

I had seen him drive by and wanted to appear distracted, unconcerned, and fully engrossed in my book. I smiled, stood up, and gave him a hug. He kissed me on the cheek like we did back then. I was shaking inside.

"What do you wanna do?" I asked him.

"Let's get a drink."

We walked up Franklin Avenue and sat on stools at an old wooden bar, staring at each other. We talked about his Fourth of July and about mine. His was clearly much more important even though he didn't tell me what had happened to him and what had landed him in the hospital. I didn't want to probe. I noticed he had dark circles under his eyes like he hadn't slept for days. He told me that he had to go on medication for depression and that he was still adjusting to the drugs. I stared at his mouth when he spoke. I wanted to kiss him, but it was crowded with all these locals, and I didn't want anyone who might know me from Milltown Tavern to see me kissing a random guy at a bar.

When we got back to my apartment, we sat on the couch and didn't stop kissing and touching each other. Nobody in the house was back from work yet, so it was dark except for the streetlights, and it was really quiet. He asked me to tell him what I wanted him to do, and I did. He carried me from the couch to my makeshift bedroom in the dining room. We took off each other's clothes, and he went down on me. We fucked slowly at first and then a little harder, because that was what I had asked.

We got dressed. He opened a big beer that he had bought at a deli on the way home from the bar. We sat on my floor, passing it back and forth. I could hear my housemates getting home from work, walking up the stairs, and going into their rooms. We slept for a few hours, and when the light came into the room, he woke up. I watched him put on his jeans. His skin was light, and his dark hair fell into his face as he bent down. I put my arms around his waist and sunk my face into his warm back.

We walked to the corner deli before he had to leave to go back to the city. I bought us each coffees and hard rolls with butter. We sat on my stoop.

"I'm gonna get pretty busy for a while, but I'll call when I can," he told me.

"That's cool."

I wanted to cry right there on the stoop because I felt rejected and lost in so many feelings. But I smiled and made out like I was totally chill about everything. He kissed me for a long time on the lips and then smiled at me. I watched him walk around the corner.

After that, I was alone. I didn't have to work for a few days. I was tempted to go stay at my moms, so I could hang out with old friends out in the suburbs, but I didn't want to answer any questions. Those people knew me too well. They would know something was up.

So, I had no choice but to be with my jagged nerves. Those hours that I spent with Shawn sunk deep into something I didn't know how to name. I wanted so much more of whatever that something was. I wanted more of him, but I knew he had pulled away from me when he left that morning. I had felt that pulling away before with guys that I liked. It was as if the more I liked them, the further away I pushed them.

I walked around in a summer haze, sitting on park benches and thinking about how happy everyone else seemed. Later, I met up with Astrid and Vera at a Cuban restaurant in Milltown. It was an old school place on a side street, an institution. There was a long counter with round stools and a few tables filled with older gray-haired Hispanic men. We sat at an outside table, drank café con leches, and smoked Camel Lights on empty stomachs.

Afterwards, we went back to Astrid's apartment, and Vera read our tarot cards. I told the two of them about Shawn and how we had slept together. They had seen me talking to him at Milltown Tavern.

We smoked some hash that Astrid scored from an ex-boyfriend out of a corncob pipe from Rite Aid. It was hot in Astrid's apartment, and her fuzzy gray cat kept crawling into my lap and digging into my bare legs.

"He's dark, that guy. Something heavy about him," Vera told me. She stared down into a bunch of cards laid out into the shape of a cross. My heart raced from the hash and her words. "But you're not done with him yet. There's more. But not all of it is good."

I was high as shit and scared but excited to know more.

"How was the sex?" Astrid asked.

"It was unreal," I said. "The best I ever had."

"You're truly fucked, girl!" Vera said, and the three of us fell to the floor, laughing.

We were pretty hash baked, so we sat cross-legged on the floor, smoked, and talked shit about Milltown Tavern people. I was curious about Rob and the kind of life he had outside of the club. Vera and Astrid had been in his intimate fold for a while.

"You just don't ever want to get on his bad side," Vera told me.

"He's a Leo," Astrid said. "He curates the people who surround him."

I told them that I had heard about the bartender who got fired because she was lovesick over a famous musician. How she tried to follow him to Seattle, only to find him ambivalent about her showing up at his door.

"He'll treat you well if he likes you. She fucked up because she got caught up with a band, and Rob hates that groupie shit," Vera said, trailing off because she got lost in her stoned thoughts.

We sat silent for a while. The sun shined bright on the hardwood floors, and a fan droned in the background. Astrid's cat was asleep on the couch.

I closed my eyes and thought about what it might feel like to be in Rob's intimate circle. I thought about Rob's success, not just as a club owner but also as someone who had so many friends. A lot of them are famous musicians, actors, and artists. I had seen how people revolved around him, how he was at the center of things, and how he was well respected. But I also knew that there was something about Rob that intimidated the shit out of me. I would get all nervy and self-conscious in his presence.

I always felt like I needed to act a certain way when he was around. Like I couldn't just be myself. I could only be the best parts of myself.

I started feeling panicky from the hash, too many cigarettes, and not enough food in my stomach. Those girls never seemed to eat. I kissed Astrid and Vera goodbye and walked through Milltown in a daze.

I stopped off for a salt bagel with cream cheese and tomato. I sat on a bench at the park and ate. It was the best bagel that I had ever had. Every piece was a magical combination of glossy cheese, crunchy salt, and sour tomato. I had a giant grin on my face, fawning over this food. I began to feel a lot better; my nerves and thoughts flowed calmly.

I walked slowly through town, toward the river. The sun was setting, and the air had cooled a bit. I was still hash high, but that was fading too, and I just felt good about where I was and what I was taking in. The people I passed were such extreme caricatures of themselves. The smells coming from the pizzeria and Dunkin Donuts could have been fake; they smelled so good. The prewar buildings looked as if they were from a movie set.

I walked and soaked in all the details, forgetting about all the stupid fucking love feelings that had been consuming the shit out of my thoughts.

I got to the river, sat on a scrubby patch of grass, and looked over at Manhattan. I was on the other side of things—the Jersey side. I always felt like I was on the Jersey side of things, like Jersey represented the lesser side. But my roots would always be in New York no matter where I ended up. New York City would be my first love because it was where my people were from and where I was born. That remained buried deep in my body. I looked uptown and thought about Shawn and how he might be copping heroin in some sketchy building. He might be sitting behind a desk at a police station. He might be in bed with someone.

It was starting to get pretty dark out. My hash buzz was gone, and things weren't feeling epic anymore. I walked fast through town. All the baseball hat guys were at the bars, all the people with money were at outdoor cafés, and all the couples were walking arm in arm down Franklin Avenue. I went back to my apartment and passed the fuck out.

* * *

It was almost midnight when Shawn came into Milltown Tavern with his cousin and one of their good friends. They came in from the city and were dressed neat with combed hair and pressed clothes.

He had called a few days prior, and we talked a bit on the phone, which helped me get by for a few days. "Things are crazy at work," he kept saying, but he'd try to come see me when he could. We didn't make plans; too much was up in the air. I pretended to be understanding, even though there was so much about him I didn't understand. I also knew there was this woman he started seeing right before me, and I had a feeling that he maybe still saw her. Maybe they still slept together. I didn't want to ask because I didn't want to know.

They were seated at a table. It was a busy night, but I kept looking over. He kept looking at me, and it felt good in a nervous way.

"You sleep with that guy yet?" Mark said, punching me in the arm.

"Shut the fuck up!"

I punched him hard back. I wanted to keep fighting with Mark because it made me feel better, but we had to keep our shit in check since Rob was on fire that night. He kept running up and down the stairs and in and out of the band room. A band called Trailer Hitch from Chicago was playing. None of us had ever heard of them, but they were fucking wild, and the energy was frenetic. When I went back to check them out and to take a smoke break, the front man was climbing up the microphone stand. The room was hot as fuck, and the crowd was raw. It was definitely one of those electric nights.

When the band finished their show, they loaded their equipment into a van. That was after most people left for the night, going back into the city, out to Brooklyn, down the New Jersey Turnpike or Route 3.

After the place was pretty much cleared out other than the usual bunch of stragglers who lurked, Pete and I had to close out the register. We counted and distributed tips to all the servers, and Mark had to clean out the litter in the band room. The cooks cleaned the kitchen, and the servers did their side work, wiping tables, putting chairs up, and filling the salt and pepper shakers. The lurkers who were allowed to hang around past closing time smoked, drank, and shot the shit.

The vibe finally chilled because Rob and Jerry Russo had both gone home. Kate was in charge of closing up, but Kate was already three Rolling Rocks deep and dancing around to jukebox music. Shawn stayed behind after his cousin and their friend left to go back to the city. He chatted mostly with my roommate Julio, who picked up server shifts every once in a while if he and Rob were getting along. In other words, if he and Rob didn't fight while doing coke together, Julio could pick up shifts for extra cash. I wasn't sure if Shawn was planning on coming home with me, but then he put his arm around me when I was in line to go to the bathroom, and I figured he would.

I could see Vera looking at us and couldn't help but think about those tarot cards and how she said Shawn would hurt me.

When it was time for us to turn off the lights and to lock the doors, I said I was going home. Shawn pushed in his barstool and followed me. Julio, Pete, and Mark stayed behind with the rest of the revelers, which meant they were going to call their dealer. I knew that would probably keep them out of the brownstone at least until the morning light.

Shawn and I walked side by side through the darkness of Milltown after the bars closed. We stopped at the pizza place by the park, the one with the dollar slices. It was bright as fuck in there. It was also full of drunken guys in baseball hats pulled down over their eyes and women who looked like they had puked or passed out already and just wanted to go home but had to wait for the guys. We got our slices and ate on the stoop of the brownstone. Both of us had a difficult time not abandoning the greasy paper plate to make out instead.

When we got inside, we didn't say shit to each other. We kissed, got ready to fuck, and fucked on and off until the blue morning light came in through the windows.

When my housemates came home the next morning, we tried to sleep but ended up sleeping and messing around on and off for most of the day. It was hot, bright, and quiet in my apartment, and it didn't matter because I didn't feel anything when I was with Shawn. I didn't feel anything emotionally, and I couldn't feel my physical body. I was hungry for him, and I wanted to be near him, but I also knew our time together was precious. It was almost like I couldn't enjoy it because I knew that soon it would be over.

He didn't end up leaving until later that evening. The sun was going down when he left, and the temperature finally cooled off. This was how he operated, similar to people getting up at sunrise except his days started when most people's days were winding down.

"We stayed in bed all day like John and Yoko," I told Mark that night after Shawn had left.

"Yeah, except at least they made music."

"Good point," I said, laughing.

We were sitting at the kitchen table, sharing a cigarette. I knew Mark was concerned for me. He wanted to be happy for me, but he couldn't be fully on board.

"I dunno… Just don't get too attached," Mark said with a pause.

"Why? Do you know something you're not telling me?" I asked him. Mt stomach tightened.

"I don't trust the guy."

He wouldn't say any more even though I tried prying the shit out of him. It wouldn't work. I had been super close friends with guys most of my life and was familiar with the emotional shutdown process. They tended to only divulge up to a certain point and then close down no matter what.

I needed to get the fuck out of the brownstone, so Mark and I walked up to Milltown Tavern for a beer. It was a Monday night, and no bands were playing, so it was pretty empty. There were only a few people sitting at the bar, and one couple was tucked away in the lounge area. We shot the shit with Kate, who was the waiting tables, and with Rafa, who was working behind the bar. I had been feeling empty and sad since Shawn had left, and I had hardly slept. I hadn't eaten all day and smoked too many cigarettes. So, I ordered a veggie burger with fries and a Rolling Rock. Just being around people made me feel not confused and sad anymore.

I had always felt confused and sad ever since I was a kid. But there was something about being intimate with Shawn and then him leaving that woke up those feelings.

I wanted to be with him in the way that normal people talked to each other on the phone before they went to bed at night. But I knew there were sharp edges around him. He didn't live a normal life. He worked a crazy risky job as an undercover cop. He had anxiety and depression, and he drank a shit ton when he wasn't working. I knew many of those things in my mind, but in my heart, I couldn't stand the thought of being rejected by him because then I would be the loser asshole that I always believed I was.

I felt a lot better on the walk home from Milltown Tavern. Mark put his arm around me and laughed at me for being so stupid lovesick over a dumb cop.

Six

Portland

After I moved out of the apartment that I shared with Paul, I rented a bedroom in a house with four, sometimes five, other roommates. The guy who lived in the basement toured with his band a lot, so he came and went. It was cheap. I wasn't either emotionally or financially equipped to live alone. My brother had sent me some funds to hold me over until I found work. A chunk of that went right away to the divorce paperwork, and then there was the room deposit, the rent, and the bills.

I was back on The Ramen Plan for the rest of the winter months. I was okay with it. I didn't want to lean on Paul for financial support. I wanted a clean break, and it felt good to be free. Paul kept the car, and I gave him most of our furniture and household shit. I took the bus, biked, or walked everywhere, which allowed me the space that I needed to be in own my head.

More than anything, I wanted to start over. I didn't want to be reminded of how I fucked up that marriage. How I was such a fucked up asshole. How I hurt him.

It was like I was suddenly back in Milltown again, moving to a new home with nothing but a futon, some clothes, and a few boxes of books. I recruited Dana to help me move. I was finishing packing up my shit, and Paul was sitting in the kitchen of our half empty apartment when she arrived. When Dana came in, I was reminded of the day she came to Milltown with a few boxes for Paul and me to bring out to Portland. She was deep in the throes of a breakup at the time. I was excited at the prospect of moving across the country and couldn't understand how she could feel so despondent. But now I understood.

"I'm gonna have a baby someday," he said to Dana. "But not with Ana."

"Uh. Okay, Paul," she said.

She and I both laughed out of awkwardness. I knew that Paul had come slightly unhinged by the move. It was a big box of triggers for both of us really. Although, I could tell that he was ready to move on too. He had started dating; we spoke about it openly. He wanted to get the normalcy back, like when he and I were still together, and he was actively seeking a stable relationship. I would never give him a stable life with a baby because I was the farthest thing from a stable person.

It was sad as fuck to leave Paul sitting alone in that apartment. I didn't think there was anything that resembles the grief of moving out from a failed relationship. It was pissing rain, of course. Dana and I were both soaked to the bone and shivering as we loaded the boxes into the car. Paul made himself scarce. Eventually, he came out, and we hugged super tight in the doorway while Dana sat in the car.

"I wish it was different, Paul," I told him. "I wish it didn't happen this way. I mean that…"

Paul needed the car back. And I really wanted to get the fuck out of that apartment and away from Paul before I broke down completely. "Let me go unload this shit real quick. We'll talk soon. Okay?"

He didn't say anything. He just closed the door behind me.

I wanted to collapse to the ground.

When I got into the car, Dana was sitting in the passenger seat, staring through the windshield. She didn't have to say anything. I knew that she knew how intense it was to break up, to move out, and to physically move on. We were in a sacred club together, and that is what trauma bonded us in those days. We drove the few miles to North Portland in silence.

* * *

It felt like I was moving to a whole different city. There were all these big, gorgeous old homes on the block, but many of them were in various states of disrepair. There were no coffee shops or restaurants within walking distance. It was quiet and a bit dodgy, and because of that, it was cheap living out there.

I had found the room to rent on a flyer at the smelly coffee shop on Alberta Street. I didn't know what the fuck I was going to do or where I was going to move. I had limited resources and no job. I had gotten to the point where I figured that I'd leave Portland and move back to Milltown, back to the brownstone, and back to Milltown Tavern. But then I was sipping coffee and looking for a job in the paper when I just happened to look up at the corkboard by the bathroom. The flyer showed a black and white photo of a small room with a big window. In scrappy handwriting, it said, "Looking for a cat friendly, somewhat neat, and super open-minded housemate in a big old house with a nice front porch. Ask for Mateo."

On the third ring, a guy picked up the phone. I told Mateo that I was calling about the room, and he said that he had to leave for work soon, but I could come right over if I wanted. He gave me the address and said me what bus I could take from Alberta Street. I was ambivalent on the bus ride over. I didn't think that the first place that I looked at would actually work out.

He had put up a big pot of herbal tea, and we sat at a wooden dining room table and chatted like we were old friends. He told me that he had moved to Oregon about a year prior from Minneapolis. He had bought the house with cheap from money he inherited from a grandparent. He had been fixing it up by himself little by little when he had extra money.

I looked around as he spoke. I could definitely see that there were things that had been replaced or repaired. There was a lot of painting patchwork and some raw, untreated wood in places. A few of the doors were off of their hinges and leaning against the walls.

Mateo had stringy, long brown hair and wore polyester pants and a threadbare white T-shirt. He had unbelievably clear blue, trusting eyes. I felt like I could tell him anything and he wouldn't judge me. He said that he worked overnights at a group home for disabled adults. He was good at getting a positive vibe from people because he went to school to be a social worker.

I told him that I had just left a relationship and was in between jobs, but I had financial help from my family.

After we drank some tea, he gave me a tour of the house. It reminded me a lot of my friend's uncle's place that I had visited one time on a road trip to Vermont. Theirs was a big, old Victorian with a giant farmhouse table and bushels of herbs drying upside down from the ceiling in the kitchen. I remembered sitting down in that house and not wanting to ever get up.

After he showed me around the first floor, I followed him up a creaky set of wooden stairs. We stood side by side in an empty bedroom. He was tall and lanky, and he towered over me, but I didn't feel intimidated by him at all.

"Hang out by yourself for a bit. Walk around the house and get a vibe."

"Okay. Thanks…" I said.

He turned and walked back downstairs. I sat on the floor in that empty room and knew immediately that I wanted to live there. It felt chill and safe. The room was small but had two long windows and a big oak tree right outside. The wooden floors showed their age, which I liked. It reminded me a lot of my room in the brownstone in Milltown. There was a lot of character and life.

I milled around the upper floor and peered into the two other bedrooms. They were messy, unkempt, and had different brands of funky smells. Mateo lived in the big attic, which was accessed by a short ladder. I climbed up and took a quick peek of the space. It was tidy, bright, and expansive; there was an altar in one of the corners with candles and a statue of a half elephant, half human. Next to that sat an unrolled yoga mat, and on top of that, a small round pillow.

I met back up with him downstairs in the kitchen. He was putting some soup in a mason jar, getting ready for work. A big black cat came scrambling through a flap in the back door. I lowered down to pet it, but it scurried away.

"I don't want to keep you. I know you need to go, but I would definitely take the room," I told him.

"Take a day. Sit with it. Call me tomorrow."

He walked me to the front door, and when I went to shake his hand, he slouched down and hugged me. I walked away, feeling awkward about the hug and nervous that he didn't like me enough to let me move in. But when I called around the same time the next day, he told me that he had hoped I would call and that he had been thinking I would be a good fit for the house. I would never know why he trusted me. I was a walking shit show with no job, a failed marriage, and an ambivalent lover.

* * *

When Dana and I got to the house on moving day, we set out to unload the boxes and the bags of clothing into my small room upstairs. Nobody was home. Mateo told me that he would leave a key under the front doormat.

When we got to my room, I noticed that the walls were dingy white, and there were dust bunnies on the creaky wooden floorboards. I found a broom in the kitchen and quickly swept it up while Dana had a look around the house. I started to feel freaked out and a little scared, kind of like when I was a kid and my mom didn't clean the house. But I told myself I would hang nice curtains on the tall windows, and maybe I would even paint the walls if Mateo was cool with that.

I figured I would make it work. I had always been good at making a shitty space feel comfortable.

Dana and I muscled my futon over our shoulders and plopped it down on the floor in my new bedroom with a big thump. Without a pause, we went straight to the front porch to get stoned. It was a chilly day, and my stomach felt tight from the stress of leaving Paul behind. But once the weed took effect, I felt a giant wave of relief. Dana and I sat on the musky porch couch, looking around and taking in the new surroundings. I could tell she was wishing that she were moving too, starting over. Things at the house between her and Jess had not been good. But we were too stoned, and I didn't want to get into it, so I didn't say anything. I just looked around. The trees were old, and the houses were big, ragtag, and perfectly beautiful.

"Don't you have to get the car back to Paul?"

"Holy shit!"

I dropped Dana off at home and then buzzed over, leaving the car with Paul. He grabbed the keys and didn't say anything to me. He didn't offer me a ride home. So, I walked all the way back to my new house, not giving much of a fuck about being cold and wet. I was still kind of stoned and fully relieved that part of my past was behind me.

* * *

Mateo's busted up old house held me together after Paul and I split up. The house on the leafy street with a giant slanting front porch that had two old couches and a plethora of overflowing ashtrays and empties scattered about on the battered coffee table. The house where it was either freezing cold or hot as fuck, depending on the mood of the ancient heating system. It was the two scrubby house cats that had belonged to a phantom roommate, who moved out years ago, and it was all the plants that had been left behind.

It was the dark and creaky wide plank floorboards that were always in need of a sweep. It was the kitchen, a cozily cluttered and slapdash space where someone would be frying eggs, cooking up a stir-fry, or making a pot of tea at all hours of day or night. It was the rows of spices and bulk foods in jars that lined the countertops, and it was the plastic recycling bins that sat in the mudroom that were constantly spilling over with empty beer and wine bottles. It was the vintage records and the dusty old paperbacks. It was the random housemates and the out-of-town visitors that came and went. It was the raucous potlucks.

And really, it was because I was treated with kindness and not judged. Mateo ended up being a recluse when he was home, which was something I would later find out had to do with being a social worker and how that work could be draining. Sometimes, we would have tea together, but I kept to myself and that was totally okay, because the house was a misfit halfway house. Everyone seemed to be going through a transition of some sort, whether it was a breakup, a depressive episode, or who the fuck knows what.

All I knew was that I would not have survived that first winter in Oregon without that crazy old house with the eternally muted natural light.

And then there was my relationship with Drew.

That winter was hard and dark, and Drew and I skirted around each other's emotions, avoiding anything of substance or depth. I was wrapped up with leaving Paul and how unsettling it was to move out of our apartment. Drew and I would mostly meet up at restaurants to eat and then go back to his house to have sex. A friend of his was visiting from California for most of the winter, crashing in Drew's spare bedroom, so there was distraction in the form of a third wheel. The three of us would get stoned and always kept things pretty first dimensional. I hardly ever spent the night at Drew's. I would mostly go back to my sparse bedroom and sleep like I had never slept before.

I would get up, go to a coffee shop, and tell myself that I was looking for a job. My funds were running low, and I figured I would leave soon anyhow worst-case scenario. My room was month to month. I figured maybe Portland just wasn't for me.

My brother rang me up one day to tell me that it was time to tell the rest of our family that Paul and I were divorcing. I just sat there, crying on the other end of the line.

"They need to know, Ana," he said with a firm tone.

"Fine," I said childlike.

I had been avoiding my family for months. My mother would call, and I would say that things were good. When she asked how Paul was doing, I would say he was good. My father never called me, and when I called him, he didn't ask too many questions. I avoided going back east for the holidays under the guise that Paul was super busy at work. So, months went by before all of the shame was revealed.

At my brother's urging, I wrote my parents letters, stating basic facts and eliminating emotions. We got married too fast. It was a big mistake. We were both doing fine. I met someone that I like a lot. Portland was wonderful, and I was thriving. My brother backed me up, saying that he had midwifed me through the process, that I really was fine, and that he had spoken to Paul a number of times. But breaking the news to my close friends back in Jersey was way worse than telling my family.

My friends had already witnessed the mood swings from my relationship with Len. But I made the calls one by one, and to be honest, none of them gave much of a shit. They just wanted to make sure I was okay. They felt that Paul was part of my life for such a short blip of time, and even though they were happy for me when we got together, he was a solid human. They also knew me well enough to know that I was really good at fucking things up.

Something shifted inside of me once the people in my inner life knew Paul and I were divorcing. The dark cloud still hovered over me but more at a distance. It would take many more months, maybe even a year, for me to come to terms with the raw and sharp pain of losing Paul. So, for a while, I ate a lot of carbs, got stoned, drank too much wine, and hung out with Drew. I didn't see Jess as much anymore, but I saw Dana when we were both in good enough moods, which wasn't often because she had such a hard time coping with the rain and the lack of employment.

That was my first Portland winter. Living like a monk in shared housing. Desperately trying to stay warm and dry. Constantly looking for a job that didn't seem to exist. Getting stoned on strong weed and amped up on strong coffee. Listening to way too many Elliott Smith dirges.

Eventually the onset of spring came, which was beyond fucking magical. It was as if I had been wading in a cold ocean for months and then finally got to sit on a warm dry beach. Everything came to life with the sun. There were all these colors, textures, and scents around me that I had never experienced before. People got nicer, friendlier. It was like all of Portland had been in a depression all winter and pulled out of it afterward.

I felt happy. I hadn't felt happy in a long time, if ever. But maybe it was just that dank Northwest weed.

Jersey

It was that time of year when it got dark early again and when the first cold wind came off the river. Shawn called me a few times late in the afternoon before I had to leave for work, which was when he was just getting up. We never made plans to get together. We would just chat for a few minutes about what we've been up to. I stopped looking at the door at Milltown Tavern, thinking maybe he'd roll in late at night. He hadn't come around in a few months, since summertime really. Any normal ass person would just cut off the emotional fucking attachment and chalk it up as a summer fling. Any normal ass person would realize that he was a dick for stringing me along. But I still hung onto the idea that he might actually want to be with me like we were normal, high-functioning people even though neither of us were anything close to that.

As the seasons changed from a bright warm sun to chilly nights, the obsession with Shawn slowly faded. I was ensconced in a solid crew of friends in Milltown and had a decent gig, and besides feeling completely beat down and non-datable, things weren't that bad. When my roommate Julio and his lady broke up for good after they had an all-night screaming match that sent Julio running through Milltown like a lunatic, I moved out of the dining room and into an actual bedroom with a door. Julio couldn't afford that rent on his own, so he got demoted back to the dining room.

On paper, I looked like this semi-legit adult, who paid bills mostly on time and even met friends for brunch. If I had enough money for brunch, then it appeared that things were going really fucking good for me.

There were a few more household changes in the mix. Rene was about to leave for a trip down to South America, and Mark was about to move off the kitchen floor downstairs and into the bedroom next to mine. We planned a going away party for Rene. He hadn't been home to see his family in a few years, and we were all super happy for him.

I knew Shawn's cousin knew about it through Julio, and I figured Shawn would know about it too. It gave me a glimmer of hope that he might turn up at the party. I couldn't call Shawn, because he lived with some old Polish lady in the city and didn't want anyone bothering her, so I didn't have an actual number for him. He always called me, and if he didn't call me, we wouldn't talk.

Julio, Mark, and I got the house ready for the party because everyone else had to work that night. It was a Thursday, and most people wouldn't arrive until well past midnight, after their shifts. I was a wreck, wondering if Shawn would show up. At one point while we were waiting for the first person to arrive, Mark came outside and found me on the stoop. I had put on a black shirt, tight jeans, and red lipstick, but I felt like an idiot clown.

"Can I grab a smoke?" Mark asked.

"Yeah, go ahead," I said.

He took a cigarette from my pack of Camel Lights and lit it with one hand from a matchbook.

"Come with me. I gotta pick up some wine," he said, and we got up from the stoop, smoked, and walked up the street to the liquor store.

We walked silently for a few blocks. I could feel my heart pounding, anticipating what might become of the night. An autumn chill was in the air, and the slippery wet leaves covered most of the sidewalk. The brownstones we passed were lit up with warm lights, and I could tell by peering into the living rooms which ones had families and which ones were couples or maybe even just roommates. I always envied the ones with families. I envied the charmed lives of kids who grew up in amazing old houses.

Mark stomped out his cigarette as we entered the overly lit store. "How many bottles should I get?" he asked.

"Two red and two white. People can bring their own shit," I said.

We each carried two bottles of barely drinkable wine in brown paper bags back home. A handful of people had arrived in our short absence, mostly Milltown Tavern coworkers and regulars. I avoided hellos, hightailed to the kitchen, and opened a bottle of wine.

I plopped down on the couch next to Julio. He also invited someone he was hoping would come. She was a good friend of his ex's, which was pretty awkward. She hadn't turned up yet and neither had Shawn, so we commiserated on that front for a while in the form of self-deprecating humor and cheap alcohol. It was a constant barrage of people coming up and down the stairs and onto the back patio for the next few hours as more and more people got off work.

I continued to drink wine and then made the mistake of smoking pot because it made my heart crawl into my throat every time a new head bopped up from the stairwell. In my weed and wine infused headspace, I took a minute and looked around the living room. I saw people I cared a lot about; we were a ragtag chosen family, sailing together in the same shoddy boat with just enough money to support ourselves and to eat moderately well. We lived in good enough housing, and we paid our bills most of time. We made art or talked about someday making art.

And here we were caught in this tiny blip of time that I would miss more than anything I could ever miss in years to come. What I didn't know then was that these were the salad days.

I didn't sit back on that eternal stoner couch, take it all in, and enjoy every minute. Because like every other love-obsessed, twenty-something asshole, I waited and waited for an unavailable fucking person to come waltzing up the creaky stairwell.

* * *

It was early morning, and a few of us were sort of cleaning up the apartment. I had smoked too many cigarettes and so much pot, and I had drunk a lot of wine. My head felt like a cotton ball that had caught on fire hours ago. Rene was passed out on the couch, snoring. In a few hours, he would have to board a plane for Caracas. I had already moved into his room upstairs, so his backpack was perched in the hallway. I looked down and envied him. There was this glimmer of hope to his narrative, reuniting with his family and then traveling for months. He had nothing but a few T-shirts and pocketful of cash to his name.

The phone rang.

"Hey," Shawn said.

"Oh, hey—" I said and tried to say more, but he interrupted me.

"I'm sorry I couldn't come earlier. I'm by the bodega near your house. Can I come over?"

"I guess. Yeah. Okay," I said. My hands shook as I set down the phone.

I ran down the stairs, and we hugged in the doorway. His face was gaunt, and his clothes were slightly disheveled. He told me that he was still in his undercover gear, the addict makeup and the ratty clothing that he put on when he went to buy heroin. When we got upstairs, he immediately hid his gun under the couch cushions and went to the bathroom to wash the makeup off of his face.

Julio, Mark, Pete, and Pete's girlfriend were milling about the apartment. Mark poked me in the ribs when he saw Shawn. We all gathered around the dining room table, smoked cigarettes, and opened a few beers. Pete put on a Polvo album. Once it started getting a little light outside, everyone said goodnight even though it was the morning. Shawn and I went upstairs.

I sat on the edge of the futon for a while, not wanting to say anything. I was still pretty wasted, and my feelings were twisted up, conflicted. I was relieved to see him, but I also felt bitter that he hadn't been in touch in a while. He came over, sat next to me, and rubbed my back.

"How did the party go?" he asked.

"Pretty fun, I guess," I said even though I hardly remembered the night.

"Yeah. I wanted to get here earlier. But things got crazy at work, and I'm having a really hard time with the meds. All I want to do is sleep all..." he said, trailing off and looking down at the floor between his feet.

I had just moved upstairs during the past week, and my room was sparse. I didn't have curtains on the windows, and my books and CDs were stacked up on the floor. But the bed was made. He kissed me, and we absorbed into each other's bodies like we were starving. Again, I lost track of time, lost in the only thing he had to offer.

When afternoon arrived, a big fog bank of heaviness and unknowns flooded my room. We fucked again. This time was fast and hard. The tension of what I was feeling had become deep and needy. I needed relief, and he gave it to me in all those sad, beautiful ways.

The house was silent in a haphazard post party kind of way. Glasses were piled on the counter; dishes and detritus were strewn about. I brewed a pot of Café Bustelo and warmed some milk in a small pot on the stove. We sat at the table, smoking and drinking strong coffee. I felt fatigued and nervy. The sun was filtering through the big windows. My body felt raw from fucking away my desperation.

I walked Shawn downstairs and onto the stoop. When the air and the light hit my skin, I retracted into myself. I knew in my body that we wouldn't keep doing this. I knew I would not see him again, not like this at least. I could tell he was somewhere far away. I figured it was his meds, his depression, and his scary, fucked up job. We didn't have to say goodbye. We didn't have to say anything because when I fucked someone a certain way, and when I grasped and clawed, there were no words.

I didn't watch him turn the corner. I sat on the stoop, put my arms around myself, and shivered.

On my way back upstairs, I noticed the door to Pete's apartment was cracked open. He heard me and came out, brushing the hair out of his eyes. We nodded at each other. I peered in and could see his girlfriend buried under the covers of their futon. "That must be nice," I said to myself. It must feel safe. I had never felt safe. I had parents who loved me but who didn't take good care of me because they didn't take good care of themselves. They didn't know how.

"You have coffee made?" Pete asked.

"Yeah. There's a little left. Come up."

He grabbed a pack of Marlboro Reds, a lighter, and a CD with a handwritten sleeve from his bedroom. I went upstairs and sat down on the couch. When Pete came up, he put on the CD. He went into the kitchen, poured himself a cup of black coffee, lit a cigarette, and sat at the table. The music was moody and unrecognizable. It paired well with the layer of sadness because our housemate and his giant backpack were now gone from his hermitage on the couch.

"He must have left super early," I said.

"I was outside smoking when he took off down the street like an urban hiker," Pete said, laughing.

I didn't know Rene that well, but we were starting to get to know each other before he left, and I began to enjoy his quiet company around the apartment. He worked in the kitchen at Milltown Tavern. He always went in to prep early in the day and then left early in the night, so we had different schedules. On his days off from the bar, he helped a friend with construction work. He wasn't the type of person to hang around the bar after shifts, and he would never spend money to go out. He bought cheap used paperback books and simple food to cook if he wasn't working in the kitchen that day. It seemed liked he would mostly eat at work. I knew he was a traveler. He worked months at a time, and when he had enough money for a trip, he left and didn't come back until all of that money was gone.

We had started sharing pots of coffee in the morning and talking about our mutual interests. Rene was a tall, soft-spoken guy with a shock of super dark hair that he kept short. He had a ruddy face that made it seem like he had been through some shit. We spoke about how I was taking creative writing, film studies, and philosophy classes in college but didn't know what I wanted to do with my life yet. How I really just wanted to watch movies and read books. How some nights I would come home super late at night from work and manically scribble poems into my journal.

"Maybe you're a writer," he said to me one morning.

"Yeah. I don't know," I said.

"You just don't know it yet. You'll know some day."

I could never be good enough to be a writer. It was not just that I would never be a good enough writer, but that I was simply not good enough of a person to be a writer. I could tell that Rene was feeling what I was feeling. He knew things about me that I didn't know because he was tuned into something bigger. He was older, wiser, and traveled. We spoke about the kinds of books that he read, mostly political. We talked about ideas and theories that I could never grasp or at least I thought I could never grasp.

"I'm gonna miss my talks with Rene," I said to Pete.

"Me too. He'll come back," he said.

"Hey, I like this music. Who is it?"

"He's this guy from Portland. Elliott Smith," he said.

"Where'd you get it?"

"Some music industry guy came into Milltown Tavern last week and left the demo at the bar for Rob, and he let me borrow it," Pete told me.

Pete and I started firing off lines from Gus Van Sant's *Drugstore Cowboy*, a movie that we both loved and talked about all the time. It took place in Portland. I couldn't imagine what it would be like there for real. It seemed so far away and stuck in a vintage sepia-toned time warp. The music Pete was playing reconfirmed the vibe.

Not long after, Mark came down bleary-eyed and busting on Pete and me for listening to such sad-sack music. He put on another pot of coffee, and we sat around the table. We didn't talk about my night with Shawn. There was nothing to say. It just didn't matter anymore, and we all knew that.

"Let's go eat," Pete said.

"Fuck yeah. Where should we go?" I asked.

"Let's just hit the diner," Mark said.

The three of us waited on the stoop for Pete's girlfriend to get dressed, and then we left the brownstone together, walking through crisp, sunny Milltown to the diner.

We passed the buildings that have stood for over a hundred years. We passed the small businesses with their dated signs and their ripped awnings. The Italian specialty shop had slabs of meat in the windows. The Chinese takeout had the bright lighting. The dusty sporting goods store smelled like rubber when I walked by. The corner market had overloaded shelves. The pizza parlor had a dark dining room in the back. And the bars. All of the bars.

In the years to come, these places would slowly peel away, only to be replaced by sleek, modern, upscale emptiness. But back then, they were locked in time, held together by family and community.

It was just another day in Milltown. Soon, it would be just another night. We would go to work in a few hours. We would pour beers for people, we would wipe tables, and we would go into the band room to smoke and to listen to live music. We would watch Rob from the corners of our eyes as he watched us from the corners of his eyes. We would try hard not to fuck up. When the night would come to an end and once the bands were breaking down their equipment and loading up their vans, we would pocket the tips that we needed to live on. We would either sit around the bar past closing, or we would go to someone's apartment. Maybe a few people would end with a tragic nightcap of coke and a jagged conversation.

No matter what and no matter how hard I tried to stop it, we would scurry off like rats to our separate lives once the sun would start to come up.

And yet our lives were not so separate.

Seven

Portland

After the rain had finally let up, and the sun came out more, I got a job working with a friend of Drew's named Tim. I was literally down to my last twenty when I got the call that I would start working again. He ran an annual independent music festival in Portland; he booked the bands and did all the coordination and promotion.

"It's a shitload of grunt work. I just want you to know before you commit," he said. "The last person I hired thought they would be hanging out with the bands."

We were in a minimal, well-designed space with stark white walls and a shiny concrete floor. It was an office party for an architectural firm in Southeast Portland. A DJ was spinning ambient music, and I could tell some people had taken ecstasy. I recognized the wide grins, the freaky pupils, and the long hugs that I knew all too well from the raver apartment days in Milltown. A handful of people with perma-smiles and dressed in trendy office attire were trance dancing.

I chatted with Tim for a while. Both of us sipped red wine out of small, clear plastic cups. I found him slightly intimidating in a privileged, liberal arts educated kind of way. He told me that he had grown up on Long Island, and after graduating from college in upstate New York, he moved to Brooklyn with a few friends. He interned at a few record labels and went out to shows more nights than not.

I had met a lot of guys like him at Milltown Tavern: balding, dark glasses, and button-down plaid shirts.

When I told him that I had bartended at Milltown Tavern and how I had worked with Rob at his label, he said he had been working on finding the funds to hire an assistant. The festival was starting to grow, and he also booked bands for a few of the clubs in town, so maybe I could end up helping with some of that stuff too.

He knew from Drew that I had left Blatant Design and that I needed a job. He also knew why and didn't seem to judge me. We spoke about NYC music venues: Knitting Factory, Irving Plaza, and Sin-e. We even talked about the Wetlands. Tim said that he had gone to a lot of shows at Milltown Tavern.

"Were you at Flaming Lips?" I asked.

"Fuck yeah, I was at Flaming Lips! That was the sickest show ever!" Tim said enthusiastically and then trailed off into his own memory bank.

"Then I probably poured you a beer," I said.

We chatted a bit longer about shows, and then I gave him my phone number. But like everything else in Portland, it took a while for him to reach out. I had to borrow more money from my brother. When I would check in with Tim over email, he would tell me that he was still waiting for budget approval from the magazine that sponsored the festival. It felt like he was just putting me off. I felt like an asshole for bugging him. I continued to look for other jobs. I had even interviewed at a boring design agency but nothing ever came to fruition.

Again, I considered moving back to Jersey. I figured I could return back into the Milltown Tavern fold. But I didn't go anywhere.

Tim stopped by Drew's one Saturday evening. We hung out in the kitchen, drinking beers. I didn't say anything about the job even though I couldn't stop thinking about it. Before he took off, Tim told me we should chat that following week. I wanted to scream or hug him, but he was super casual about the whole thing.

"Oh, okay. Did the budget get approved?" I asked.

"Fucking finally," he told me.

It took another few weeks, but I was eventually hired. We worked out of a dusty office space in an old factory building in Portland's Southeast Industrial area, near Willamette River. Most days, Tim wouldn't turn up until late in the afternoon. I took the bus from North Portland and let myself into the office. Sometimes, I rode my bike.

I felt this sense of wholeness as if I had purpose again. There was routine, a rhythm to my days.

The pay wasn't amazing, but I had more than enough to get by on, enough that I didn't have to call my brother for any more money. I got to work with bands again too. But after that morning caffeine jolt turned from inspiration to desperation, I felt super empty. For the first time since moving out to Oregon, I felt homesick. I missed my crazy family. I missed my vast assortment of friends, the people who truly knew me. I missed New York City. I even missed dumb ass Jersey!

I couldn't believe that I was married and living on a different coastline a year ago.

All the feelings came at me at once. For some reason, a bunch of shit got kicked up with all the dust in that old building. It was probably because I was forced to be alone. I had to face all those feelings and could no longer hide in the wine, the weed, and the hippie house, or with the somewhat distant lover. I had to sit in a thrown together office with a big overstuffed couch, concert posters, and an untrustworthy fax machine.

* * *

I had hardly slept at all the night before. It had gotten hot, and my room felt like an oven. The thing about it getting hot in Portland was that not everyone had air-conditioning like on the east coast. Even though it didn't get crazy hot that often, when it did, I had no choice but to suffer through it. Everything slowed down to a strange halt. So, I was in this deep, spaced out fog when I got to the office from lack of sleep and the oppressive heat. I got an iced coffee and made it through the morning.

We had a freelance graphic designer in for the week, producing posters and ads for the festival. His name was Chris. He was a quiet, nerdy guy in his early thirties with a shaved head and wire-framed glasses. He worked super efficiently, so I hardly had to wrangle him at all. Really, I just had to answer questions, send emails, or make calls if he needed information on dates, a band, or a venue. Mostly, he sat in front of his screen with headphones pinned to his ears, and when I would sidle up next to him, he would pull one out to the side.

He had a funny, dry sense of humor, so every once in a while, we would crack a joke and laugh, which broke through some of my existential grief and weariness.

"Yo," he said, walking in the door. His bike clicked away at his side.

"What's up?" I asked.

"Oh man. I hardly slept last night. It was super fucking hot in my house. My cat was freaking the fuck out," he said.

"Tell me about it. I was losing my mind," I said, and we laughed.

He had grown up somewhere in the Midwest, where it would get superhot and humid in summer like it did in Jersey, and we commiserated on the lack of air-conditioning in Portland. It was way too easy to hate on Portland, especially since we weren't from there.

We sat at our desks, drank iced coffee, and panted. He put on his headphones and worked on some layouts. I stared at my computer and tried my best to craft a few semi-legible emails. We had to send some files to the printer by the end of the day, so a deadline was looming. Tim was planning on coming in to give his final okay.

I hadn't seen Paul in a while. Although, I had heard from Dana that he was dating someone seriously. I would have been okay continuing to hang out as friends, but he wouldn't have it, and I had no choice but to let it be.

He was now my ex-husband. When I told people I had an ex-husband, it shocked them. When I told them that we were only married for nine months, it shocked them even more. I felt like an idiot saying these things, but I couldn't lie. It mostly came up when someone would ask how I ended up in Portland. I started saying ex instead of ex-husband, because with husband came shock and a blanket of shame.

Everyone had an ex and had been through a breakup, but not everyone in their twenties had already been married and divorced.

I was starting to feel strong again, semi-grounded. I had an okay job and a decent place to live. I was in a relationship that was emotionally detached but kind of sweet, and even though I probably should have been alone after I left Paul, I didn't have it in me to be alone. I still didn't know too many people in Portland. Drew was this temporary anchor that kept me from drifting back home to Jersey. As much as I pined to return to home, I knew there was still something left for me in Portland.

I hadn't even given Portland a full year yet. I wasn't about to turn back to Jersey like Dana did. She had given up and left rather abruptly. She called her mom one day to complain about being crazy broke, and her stepdad basically bought her a plane ticket home for the following week. It was hard to see her go because she was my remaining connection to Jersey. I didn't spend any time with Jess anymore. I lost Jess when I left Paul.

The night before Dana flew out, we sat on my porch and smoked. She was shaky and manic, talking about all the epic art she was going to make when she got back to Milltown.

Something about her was gone, kind of like when she was about to move out to Portland.

I went outside to the old storage building to smoke. I was covered in a layer dust from the building and sweat from the oppressive heat. There was something to the raw grit of sitting on a curb under a bridge, surrounded by homeless encampments and passing skateboarders with their T-shirts tied to their heads. I laughed at myself for always being drawn to urban decay. It was midday, and the sun was shining down on the cobblestone street, surrounding the building and producing this vibrant, orange color. It reminded me of wandering around lower Manhattan in the middle of summer.

The sun's orange color. The cobblestone. That familiar layer of dried sweat and grime.

I sat on the curb for a few minutes, smoking and thinking. Maybe I'd make a trip back to Jersey after the musical festival was over. Autumn was my favorite time of year back east. I would talk to Tim about it soon. I could even work a bit from there, making calls and answering emails. Maybe I'd even go to some shows. Maybe Drew would come too, and we could walk around the city together.

By the time I got upstairs, I was feeling a little better. Hopeful. Chris stood in front of a large fan that was on full blast. His shirt billowed.

"You ready to show Tim the files?" I asked him.

"Yeah. I gotta get out of here though. It's too fucking hot. I can't think straight."

"Let's grab lunch, and then we can come back and meet Tim to go over shit," I said.

We were out of that office and on the stairwell in a matter of seconds. There was a diner a few blocks away. It was way cooler than the office that's original intention was to hold things and not people. We ate turkey clubs and shared a plate of fries.

I told Chris that I was thinking about heading back east for a bit to see my family and some friends. He told me that the first time he went back to the Midwest, after he moved out to Portland, messed with his head. Every time he went back, he questioned why he left. He ended up drinking too much with his old friends from high school and falling back on old patterns. When he came back to Portland, he felt a great sense of relief.

"Are you close with your family?" I asked him.

"In a way, yeah. But I think having this distance is better for us. We talk more. My parents aren't up my ass like they were when I lived home. They don't worry as much. Like now they can just let me live my life."

"I like that," I said and thought about my own family, my own life.

"Were you a fucked-up kid?" I asked.

"Uh. You could say that."

He told me that his parents divorced when he was little and that his mom was an alcoholic. She would drink white wine in a nice glass like she was fancy, but it was cheap wine, and she drank a lot of it. She would pass out on the couch every night after dinner. When he was a teenager, with the same amount of energy it took to be an alcoholic, she got into AA, which led her into becoming a born-again Christian.

"The white wine was the gateway drug," Chris told me, smiling and pausing for a minute to eat a few fries. "It was actually way better when she drank and passed out in front of the TV cause when she got crazy into the church, she wouldn't shut up about God this and God that."

"Where was your dad?" I asked.

"Who?" he asked, and we both laughed.

I told Chris about my own parents' divorce, how my father remarried a cruel, cold woman and how my stepmother only cared about the tidiness of the house. I told him how my mother didn't drink white wine or go crazy with the church, but she got depressed and never truly recovered from her divorce. I told him that I never felt like I actually had parents and how in many ways, I had raised myself. I still was raising myself.

We talked about how we would never want to make the mistake of being fucked up and self-absorbed if we ever had kids.

"That shit was way too 1980's," Chris said.

"Oh my god. It was! Everyone's parents were getting divorced and going crazy. What the fuck?" I said and looked up at the clock. "We better get back before Tim gets to the office."

We paid our check at the register and left the restaurant. It was the hottest part of the day. I was feeling kind of freaked out about talking openly about my shit childhood. I hardly ever shared that part of me with anyone. But I thought about how Chris said things with his family improved since he left home, and I felt a little better. Maybe that would happen to me. It was supposed to cool off later in the night, and I just kept thinking about going home, taking a cool shower, and hanging out alone in my room. Maybe I'd even see Drew later.

We passed two guys with shopping carts filled with clanking cans. I had seen them together many times before and thought they may have been brothers. They both had similar long, curly blond hair and big beards, and they walked side by side, not saying anything. I felt super sad thinking of what it was like being homeless and trying to get by in the heat.

We made it back to the dusty building under the bridge. When we walked up the stairs and into the office, Tim was already there, sitting on the old couch, in the middle of a phone call. He looked pissed. My heart raced. It felt like I walked into my dad's house and didn't know what mood my stepmother would be in. But when Tim got off the phone, he was cheery. I felt relief because I wasn't in trouble.

"The poster and ad files look great, you guys! I marked up a few things. Let's get those changes made and get them off to the printer," he said.

"No worries, man," Chris said.

The festival was in a month. It was crunch time, so it wasn't a good time to talk to Tim about taking time off from work to head back to Jersey. I'd wait. I wasn't ready to go back home anyways.

Jersey wasn't going anywhere.

Jersey

I never had a strong sense of home. I never learned what it was like to feel safe in the world. I never knew what kind of person I really was. My mother was emotionally unstable. My father was focused on protecting his fragile wife like she would break, and sometimes she did. So, it was mainly down to me and my older brother. Because we were trauma bonded from years of orbiting around those two psycho worlds, there have been times that we have become surrogate parents to each other.

We midwifed each other through heart-wrenching breakups and job bullshit. We turned to each other when we didn't have the energy to turn to friends.

When I found out I was pregnant, the first person I told was my brother. We had planned to meet up at our mother's apartment, because we were going to a family gathering: a baby shower. The irony. While our mother was in the bathroom, I blurted it out. I hadn't even planned to tell him, but it just fell out of my mouth.

"I just found out that I'm pregnant," I said.

"You joking, Ana?"

"No," I told him.

"For fuck's sake…" After a pause, he said, "You must have really wanted to tell somebody."

"Don't tell Ma."

We heard the toilet flush and stopped talking. My brother was ten years older. He had been through an unplanned, unwanted pregnancy with his ex. I was a rascally teenager when it happened, but I noticed how upset he was by the whole thing. We were both pretty somber when we left the apartment and drove over to our cousin's house for the baby shower.

"You better eat extra food since you're eating for two now," my brother whispered into my ear, trying to make me laugh.

"Nice one," I said and walked away.

I felt sick, swollen, and sad. Every time I went to the bathroom, I would look for spots of blood on my underwear as if this nightmare would just end. What I didn't tell my brother and what I was having a hard time coming to terms with was the fact I didn't really know who the father was. I felt like I was going insane. How could something like this happen to me? I had slept with two people in the past month. After Sean stopped calling me, I started sleeping with the sound guy from Milltown Tavern.

Ever since I was in my teens, I felt that I would for sure get AIDS. I had tons of unprotected, risky sex when I was younger. It was not something I was proud of. So, I got into the routine of getting AIDS tests every few months.

"It's like you won't be able to relax until you get AIDS," my old friend, Rich, from high school said once.

"You know, you're probably right," I said.

"Just use fucking condoms, dude. What the fuck?"

"I don't know what the fuck," I answered.

We were at a diner. I had just gotten back from getting my quarterly AIDS test results at Planned Parenthood and was feeling uplifted by yet another negative result. I sat in a booth with a purse filled with free condoms. He was right. Why didn't I just use condoms? Well, I did use condoms. And then I didn't. I would get into a sexual relationship with someone, and we would use condoms. Then we would get AIDS tests, show each other our AIDS paperwork, and then start fucking without condoms.

I didn't think about getting pregnant. I thought about getting AIDS.

Later that night, after I got back to my apartment, I took another pregnancy test, thinking maybe it would all disappear. But it made a double line right away. "At least it wasn't an AIDS test," I said to myself while sitting in the bathroom and staring at the crumbling tile and the darkened grout. I peeled myself off the toilet and sat on the floor.

I decided I would move to California and raise this random baby. I wouldn't tell either possible dad about the kid. I wouldn't tell anyone. I would pick up a ton of shifts at Milltown Tavern, and I would leave Jersey when I had enough money to get by for a while. I would figure out a way to live as a single mom with a baby in the bright happy sun.

Solid plan, right?

* * *

After getting an abortion for the first time, nobody told me what an emotional fucking roller coaster it would be in the aftermath. Nobody told me that my body would be in shock from being pregnant one minute and not pregnant the next. Nobody told me that there would be a festering well of tremendous grief to grapple with for months, for years to come.

I found my way to the clinic in a state of suspended reality as if I had been hovering between becoming a mother and the possibility being extracted from my body like a rotten tooth. It was like nothing else in the world because the raw power that I held: my ability to one minute be a woman containing a growing fetus and then the next hiring someone to destroy that fetus. It was a witchy kind of magic.

The idea of moving to California to raise a child by myself was fleeting, lost in some sepia-toned vintage film about a pregnant runaway. I took the bus alone to the clinic, which was about a half hour ride through a dense, urban part of Jersey. It was cold out, so I wore an oversized navy-blue overcoat and sweatpants. I hadn't slept well in the days leading up to this impending procedure. The only person who knew of my condition was my brother, and even though we spoke on the phone every day, I felt alone. I would only tell friends afterward. I wasn't ready to face the shame and make it real.

There also was the other issue of the not knowing who it was that got me pregnant. During the time I was broken up over Shawn, I had a tryst with the sound guy from Milltown Tavern. We ended up hanging out one night after work. He ended coming over, and we ended up having friend sex. It was nothing more than not wanting to be alone. It was fun enough but not that fun, so it never happened again. We were okay with that.

Did we use a condom? One time, yes. One time, no.

I couldn't handle the shame of telling these two lovers that one of them was responsible, but I didn't know which one was. That felt way too fucking awkward. For a minute, I was tempted to reel Shawn back into my life by holding him responsible. The thought of him nursing me in bed after the abortion and us bonding over this severely existential experience that might bring him back into my life was also fleeting, because I knew he would again just fade away.

The clinic waiting room was almost worse than the abortion. A teenager, who looked barely fourteen with a face full of metal, was flanked by her haggard, sleep-deprived mother and a weepy, inconsolable boyfriend with stringy pink hair. A middle-aged suburbanite in a tracksuit and nice jewelry attempted to lose herself in a glossy magazine. There were so many crying babies and clingy toddlers, all of which were painful reminders that we were about to kill those chances.

When I came to after the procedure, I was given a lollipop and a fistful of antibiotics and was told that it was time to go home. I sat for a while in the sickly-lit recovery area, waiting for the meds to wear off so I could stand up and walk out of there. There were about ten women. All of us were lined up in a row of uncomfortable chairs in flimsy gowns, sucking on our lollipops like sad little children. All lost in a melancholic daze of postanesthesia.

One woman, late thirty something and Jersey style boisterous with a nest of blond hair, had opted out of general anesthesia. She bragged to the rest of us about how she'd given birth three times and that she could handle the pain. She wasn't even sucking on a lollipop. She just looked tired like she had to go home to a house full of kids and a gross husband and would rather just convalesce in the postabortion dungeon.

I felt dizzy and nauseous on the bus ride back to Milltown, especially with all of the braking and all of the stops. I knew I couldn't have driven myself, but I could have either asked someone to drive me or even taken a cab. I felt like such a degenerate asshole that I didn't want to tell anyone what was going on, and I couldn't stand the thought of being in such an intimate in a space with another person.

I wanted nothing more than to crawl into bed and not come out for a long time. I called in sick for work three straight days, telling Rob that I had the flu. He was annoyed but had no choice but to be okay with it. People fucking got sick. I thumbtacked a heavy blanket over my windows to keep out the light and fell into a deep, dark depression.

Everyone in the house left me alone as if they knew. I was like a sick animal who had gone into the woods to die alone. I subsisted on a diet of toast and cream of wheat cereal, which I took up to my darkened room and consumed in bed.

Later, I finally got out of bed and removed the abortion blanket from the window. Mark had started lurking near my bedroom door, knocking even though I wouldn't answer.

When I snapped at him to go away and that I was just sick, I knew it was time to get the fuck up and face my life.

It was a crisp late autumn day, and the sun was blaring hard into my eyes while I walked through Milltown. I had been living in a dark cave, and it hurt to be outside. Because of the cost of the abortion and the fact I had missed a few shifts, I was broke until the weekend. I borrowed a twenty from Mark after apologizing for snapping at him. I went to the Barnes and Noble in Union Square and nursed a coffee in the café. I flipped through a tattered copy of Artforum. It was complicated being back in the world again, and even though I was tempted to go back to my blanket cave, I headed downtown instead to hopefully catch a sad foreign film at the Angelika Film Center, perfect medicine for my condition.

But then I saw Shawn cross Houston. Maybe I was hallucinating, but I swore it was him.

He wore his usual black on black, smoking a cigarette and walking with his head down. At first, I was just going to keep heading toward the theater, but I felt compelled to follow him. I crossed Houston and headed onto Soho. This person had dominated the shit out of my consciousness for a long time, but I didn't really know him. I had never been to his apartment, and even though I knew his cousin, I didn't know much about his family. And he may or may not have gotten me pregnant.

My body ached from getting gutted. I felt raw and exposed. I was shelled.

I caught up to him in front of a deli off of Greene Street. I waited outside while he bought a coffee. And then there I was, standing on the sidewalk like a fucking stalker.

"Holy shit, Ana," he said, startled.

"Sorry. I saw you walking from a few blocks away…"

He put his coffee on the ground and hugged me hard. I wanted to tell him everything. How I had been needy. How I wanted him to be something that he wasn't: emotionally available and actually wanting to commit to a relationship with me. How I slept with the sound guy and then found out I was pregnant.

I wanted to tell him that I was ashamed about what happened. I dealt with it by myself. But I didn't say anything to him about it. We just walked a few blocks together and sat on a metal grate in front of the Soho art gallery.

It was a quiet cobblestone street. Just a few people sat at desks in sparse art galleries and tended to retail shops with minimal inventory. A tall, painfully skinny woman in leather pants, who may or may not have been a model, walked by with a black standard poodle. She probably had an abortion.

A man sat in at a box truck, writing on a clipboard. Sean and I smoked and just sat there, not saying much.

"You seem bummed," he said.

"Yeah. I got really sick last week and had to stay in bed for a few days."

"That sucks."

"I put a blanket over my window," I told him.

"You got depressed?"

"What do you mean?" I asked.

"That's what depressed people do."

He offered me a sip of his coffee. It was cold on the metal grate. I was shivering, and he put his arm around me and rubbed by back. I drank the warm coffee and stared up at the lofts with the floor to ceiling windows. I thought about what it would be like to live in one of those places. If I could actually afford one, if I was a real working artist, I would be happy. I would share it with a partner. We would make pots of stovetop espresso in the morning and read at a chunky wooden farmhouse table with mismatched chairs. Then we would retreat into separate studios at the back of the loft to tend to our work until evening, whenever that would be. My family would be proud of me. They would think I was a successful person. I would host family dinners, and then later in bed, my partner and I would laugh about how crazy our families were, how different we were from those nutty people.

In other words, I wouldn't be a bartender working toward a useless philosophy degree who lived with a pile of scrappy people in a rundown brownstone in Jersey. I wouldn't be the kind of person who would be sitting postabortion with the person who may or may not have been one who impregnated me. I would never hang a heavy blanket from one of those amazing windows, because I would not want to keep out the gorgeous light.

"I gotta go. I'm going to see a depressing movie," I said.

"Oh, yeah? I'm not into those kinds of movies," he told me.

"Then, I'll see you later," I said.

"Yeah, you will."

We hugged quick and disconnected. Something was gone. While walking down the block and heading toward the theater, I laughed at myself because I could never be with a person who didn't like depressing movies.

“Fuck that guy,” I said out loud as I crossed Houston, because I could do that in the streets of New York City.

Eight

Portland

The musical festival came and went. I worked really hard on this one thing for a while and then suddenly I was sitting at my desk with no emails to answer and no calls to respond to. Nobody wanted anything from me anymore. But it all came at a good time because during the time that I was in the weeds at work, I had clearly needed a break from thinking about how I had fucked shit up so hard. I was beat down from beating myself up. I was sick of being homesick for Jersey. I was done with pining for some kind of psychic change to suddenly appear out of nowhere.

So, once the quiet hit at work, I moved myself into Drew's.

Things at the groovy group house had fallen apart. The guy who rented the basement room and who had been on tour with his band was suddenly home all the time. The band had broken up, and he—James—had nothing else to focus on: no job, no relationship, no nothing. He was clearly dealing with some heavy personal demons, so he began micromanaging shit around the house.

It started when Mateo began dating this woman with blond, waist-length dreadlocks. She would tuck it up in a big beehive on top of her head. Something about her overall vibe and bodily funk threw the house flora off balance. She spent most nights up in the loft with Mateo and most days splayed out in the window seat downstairs, scribbling in a cloth-bound journal and talking in a creepy childish voice to the cats.

But beyond the funky dreadlocks, which I would think was the most obvious trigger, I could tell that James didn't like the whole freeloading aspect. I didn't like it either, but it was Mateo's house, and he made all the decisions. I also had started spending more nights at Drew's, and I gave almost zero fucks what anyone did in that house.

This was clearly something that James was not used to. He started to laser focus on those dumb dreadlocks.

"White people are not meant to have dreadlocks," he said to me in the kitchen one morning. "I have lived for weeks at a time in a van with disgusting musicians, and nothing reeks as bad as—"

"Oh man," I said.

"And she doesn't contribute shit. She sleeps here, she eats here, and she shits here. She leaves her dishes in the sink!"

"Yeah, but this is Mateo's house, and I don't think—"

"I can't live this this. I just can't. We need to come together and let Mateo know how we feel," James said, clustering me into his drama.

"Listen, man. I gotta get going. Let's talk about this later," I said.

I went upstairs to plot a way out of this psycho situation. There was no rationalizing with James; I knew this firsthand from growing up with a control-freak stepmother. It would be all about him and only about how he felt. He would never be able to fully take in another person's perspective. There was no chance of politic with that guy. He was reeling from the breakup of his band and was making something out of nothing in order to not face his own shit.

It had been way chill at the house before James came back from tour. And as long as he was going be around more, the solace would be gone. If it wasn't the case of the stinky dreadlocks, it would be something else.

I sat for a while in my room, sketching out some ideas in a notebook. I looked at how much Tim was paying me and what type of living situation I would be able to afford.

I could always form an alliance with our other housemate, but Sarah was this quiet-as-a-mouse type who worked long hours at a nonprofit. I knew she avoided conflict of any sort by getting all academic and brainy, theorizing the shit out of any disruptions in the house equilibrium. I witnessed it once when there was an issue around toilet paper. She felt she was the only one buying it, and even though Mateo attempted to salve her concerns by putting a rotating toilet paper purchasing chart up in the kitchen, she wasn't having any of it.

She even scheduled a house meeting. We all sat at the dining room table and listened to her throw down a feminist theory about how so much of the domestic labor falls solely on women. She passed around a book and asked us to only use this nonviolent communication tactics in our dialogue. It was exhausting watching her proselytize, and luckily, I was a little stoned, so it was also a little entertaining. I ran right over to Drew's afterward and debriefed him on his front porch.

After that, I bought toilet paper every few weeks, and I stayed away from Sarah as much as possible. I started staying at Drew's a lot more too. It didn't take me long to realize that if I opened up any kind of dialogue with her around the stinky dreadlock debacle, she would draft up a fucking syllabus with a required reading list. Fuck that.

My only choice was to move out, but I didn't know where I would go. I didn't have the bandwidth to deal with another commune flare. I didn't have enough money for my own place. My only choice was to move into Drew's. When I brought it up, he was super apprehensive and freaked out. I had no other choice but to force him into it, which was something that would come crashing down on me later.

When I told him I was moving out, Mateo was cool because he was blissed out and in love. He was super positive and not really dealing with the true shit, which was something I would come to terms within the months following. I had thought Mateo was this smart, insightful, and kind-hearted person who had traveled a ton and who had studied with a Shaman in Costa Rica. But in reality, he was a total avoidant, wearing the mask of someone who was enlightened. The more I lived in Portland, the more these types of people came out from under mossy rocks.

I figured living with Drew would be safe, an escape hatch from these undercover narcissists.

* * *

We moved everything in Drew's Passat wagon. He seemed unmoved by the move. He was ambivalent. I basically unpacked my things in his guest room, and we kept the rest of his house intact as if his independence needed to be staged. His buddy who was staying there through the summer had just moved back to California, so there was a shift in energy around the house.

It was Labor Day Weekend. After we got back from moving the last of my things, Drew went out skateboarding with a friend. I had started noticing that that was what he did when he needed to clear his head. I got high, put on New Order's *Substance* on the CD player, and cleaned the shit out of the house. It was my way of claiming the space like a dog pissing on a tree. It probably hadn't been cleaned properly since Drew moved in a few years prior. I put my clothes away in the guest closet. I stacked my books on a bookshelf in the second bedroom.

I couldn't say I felt at home, but it felt a lot better than walking around on eggshells.

When Drew came home, I made a stir-fry. A co-op grocery store had just opened up a few blocks away on Alberta Street. I had walked over earlier to buy some things: ginger, garlic, carrots, broccoli, spinach, tofu, and rice for the stir-fry. I also got some morning basics like granola, milk, bread, eggs, and coffee. I loved the smell of the co-op, all the bulk spices, teas, and natural products. It reminded me of the old hippie grocery stores in the East Village that I would wander into and never know what to buy.

"Did you clean?" Drew asked, walking into the living room.

"Yeah. Can you tell?"

"It looks good. Wow!" he said, walking into kitchen. "You bought food too!"

"Um, yeah. This is what you do when you live like a normal person," I said, jokingly.

I had cooked for Drew at his house many times before, but something about the cleaning and the cooking together shifted something in him.

We ate with chopsticks. We shared a beer. He looked out the window by the kitchen table, and then he looked back at me. He smiled a little and sunk down into his chair.

"What?" I asked, wondering what he was thinking about.

"Nothing."

"Are you sure you are okay with this? With me being here? It could just be a temporary thing. We talked about that. I had to get out of—"

"It's okay. We'll see," he said, cutting me off.

He didn't want to talk about it. He didn't want to acknowledge that he had a girlfriend living with him for the first time. I knew not to press him any further because that would be too close to the edge of intimacy. I had learned that he was hard to get to know. He had been my lover for six months. We had spent many days and nights together. But we had kept each other at a distance, and now we were living together.

I figured I could always just stay until I found another place to live. I could start looking for a better paying job, and then I could afford my own apartment. That would be my plan. King of like when I moved into Mateo's house—a temporary bridge in a housing gap.

* * *

Drew was still sleeping when my phone rang. I had been living at his house for just over a week.

"Ana, have you seen the television?" my mother asked.

"No. Why? What, Ma?"

"Just look, honey. It's just awful. Your brother is fine..."

I didn't know what the fuck she was talking about. My mother was obviously panicked. But I was used to her being panicked for no reason at all. I sat on the couch and held the remote in my hands. My heart raced. I kept the phone by my ear and turned on the television.

Then I saw the footage: burning towers and the insane chaos of lower Manhattan.

The first person I thought of when I got off the phone was my brother. He lived in Queens but worked in midtown Manhattan. My mother said he had called her from a restaurant in the city, where he was holed up with some friends from work. He didn't know how he would get back to Queens since the trains weren't running, but he said he was okay.

Then I thought about Paul. Before we moved out west, we had lived together right across the river from Manhattan. We'd often take the train into the city and hang out by the World Trade Center. Sometimes, we'd take our bikes on the ferry and ride around the city. He came from where I came from. Out roots were entangled, and our families and a lot of our friends were still back there. We both knew people who worked in Manhattan.

I didn't know what to do with myself. I wanted to start making calls, but I was frozen. Drew overheard me talking to my mother and got up to see what was going on. I just pointed at the television. We sat on the couch for most of the morning.

I could have called in sick for work, but I didn't want to stay home. Before I went into that storage building, I tried calling my brother and a few friends, but my cell service wasn't working. I broke down and called Paul. We hadn't spoken in months.

"Hey. It's Ana," I said when he picked up.

"Oh. Hey."

"Are you okay? Is everyone okay?"

"Everyone's fine," he said dryly.

It was obvious he didn't want to talk. I had felt such a strong need to connect with him after the towers fell that day, but it was obvious he didn't feel that need to connect with me. We had left together, we had broken up with that city together, and now we were broken up while it was all breaking down.

I could tell that Drew was freaked out, but he didn't have the emotional connection to the city like I had. Like Paul had.

I got to work, sat outside of the storage building, and smoked. I thought about what life would have been like had Paul and I not left Jersey. Maybe we would still have been together, because in so many ways, it was New York that had held us together.

Jersey

Paul came into Milltown Tavern one night with some friends to see Mike Watt play. We had gone to the same college; I saw him often in the fine arts building. He was an assistant in the photo department. We never spoke to each other, but we knew each other.

This was how it all started with Paul.

I was still working at Milltown Tavern and taking residence in the brownstone. There had been a constant shift between housemates. Someone would move out and in with a lover, only to return again when that relationship ended. People sometimes doubled up in bedrooms. The dining room was often a converted bedroom as it was when I first moved in. Someone even slept in a hammock on the back porch for a few weeks until a bedroom was due to be vacant. Through it all, we somehow managed to keep the house in the Milltown Tavern family. It was our halfway house, but we had no idea what it was halfway toward.

"Hey, I know you," Paul said, sidling up to the end of the packed bar.

"Oh yeah? I know you too. How's it going?"

"Good. We came in from Brooklyn to see Watt," Paul said to me.

"You living out there now?" I asked.

"Yeah, we just finished renovating a loft space in Greenpoint. We're having our official housewarming next week ."

"Cool. Hey, sorry. I gotta get back to these people, but you need a beer?" I asked, handing him a Rolling Rock that I had just opened for someone else.

"Uh, yeah. Sure."

"On me."

"Wow! Thanks," Paul said.

"No problem," I said and then got right back to the busy bar.

The bar was packed with hands resting on twenties and people starting at me, pining hard for a drink. I had a long night ahead of me and was already wiped out. I had just started working during the weekdays, helping Rob with his record label. I couldn't stand serving people alcohol anymore. I was burned the fuck out. So, after a few days in the dark basement grappling with Rob and his coke-infused moods, I was worn down and aggravated. But I still needed the income I made from bartending, so I had no choice but to stick with the bar shifts.

What I really wanted was a job with a desk and a phone. Kind of like a little kid playing office. The previous spring, I had graduated from college by the skin of my ass really. When I walked into the philosophy department to have the secretary sign a form so I could graduate, it felt like she was happy to just sign off to get rid of me. I was six years in with a barely passing grade point average. But I finished, and that felt pretty good. Now, I wanted to learn about the business side of music even though Rob was hard to deal with most of the time. He was moody as fuck; there was no other way to put it.

My heart would crack open when I would think about leaving Milltown Tavern. Astrid, Vera, and Kate were my chosen sisters. Mark and Pete were my chosen pain-in-the-ass brothers. Rob and Jerry Russo were my unreliable surrogate parents. Even the door guys, the cooks, and the guy who mopped the floors were like chosen family. All with drama, disillusion, and dysfunction included.

I had finally found my people. I also knew that working at Milltown Tavern wouldn't be forever. I wanted more out of life than pouring pints and tracking down missing musicians. The other issue was that Milltown was gentrifying like a motherfucker. Even though our rent never went up, the cost of living was getting high. We never knew if our landlord would sell the brownstone, because if he did, we knew we would never be able to afford to stay in town. We'd have to go deep and cheap into thick urban Jersey.

Some of the artists and musicians who hung around Milltown Tavern had already migrated. They had moved upstate to Hudson and Beacon, down the shore to Asbury Park, and out west to Seattle and Portland. A few people were even talking about moving to Amsterdam where weed was kind of legal. I couldn't even imagine leaving Jersey.

The night Mike Watt played had an especially charged energy. It was peak autumn, and I could tell that something was about to blow the fuck apart. I would be lying to say that I didn't still pine hard for Shawn, that I didn't hope that maybe he would come back into my life again. The funny part was that he eventually did come back. But it was me who wasn't available.

After the show, Paul and his friends sat at one of Kate's tables in the café area. I stopped by to chat. It had slowed down by that point, and since I had opened the bar earlier, Pete was due to close it out. I told them that Mike Watt was lurking around the bar earlier. I told them about the night Evan Dando played. Kate had to hold him by the arm and escort him to the ATM because he was super high. I told them about pouring a beer for a guy one night and then looking up to see it was David Byrne. I told them about Beck and how he hung out before the show in the apartment upstairs, surrounded by a harem of girls who were way too young.

"So, how'd you guys score that loft in Greenpoint?" I asked.

"Cash money," Paul said.

"It's a pretty shady situation," one of Paul's friends said. "You have to pay the landlord in cash every month because it's not zoned residential. We did all the renovations ourselves. Built out bedrooms and put in a full kitchen and a bathroom."

They were dressed in crisp sneakers, button down shirts, hoodies, and thick glasses. It was clear that they were all next level money, not still scrapping check to check or shift by shift. These guys were for sure on a salary with full benefits. I wondered what it would be like to get up early in the morning like a normal-ass person, grab the subway into the city, score a paper cup of coffee at the corner deli, and then tuck into a tidy desk for the rest of the day.

"Where do you guys work?" I asked.

"In the city. I work at a photo studio, and these guys are web designers," Paul said.

"Oh cool," I said.

I still had to do a few things to close out the night. I broke away from Paul and his buddies. Kate was teaching a new server how to do all the side work, so I helped Astrid and Vera put the chairs up on tables. I counted out tips with Pete and restocked a few bottles behind the bar. When we turned the overhead lights on, it meant we were trying to get everyone the fuck out.

"Last call!" Pete yelled.

As I was wiping down the bar, Paul came over. His friends hovered in the doorway, waiting to leave.

"Cool to see you again," I said.

"Yeah, totally. Oh. Hey. Come to our housewarming party if you can. Here's my number," Paul said, handing me a folded-up piece of paper.

"Sure. I'll definitely try," I said, and we hugged awkwardly.

Paul headed toward the door, and I waved back at his friends, tucking the paper into my back pocket.

I could feel Dana, the new server, watching the whole exchange. It was an Milltown Tavern tradition for the veterans to be standoffish to new employees until they were properly indoctrinated into the family. But I liked her already. She was painfully transparent and blunt in a true Jersey fashion.

"Who's that guy?" she asked.

"Oh, I went to college with him. He was a TA in the art department."

"Of course, he was. His friends are pretty cute," she said.

"Wanna come with me to a party at their loft in Greenpoint?"

"Okay," she said.

* * *

We took the train from Milltown into the city and then headed out to Brooklyn on the subway. When we got off the train, it was a bustling Saturday night with crowded bars, restaurants, and brightly lit delis lining the avenue. There was a vibe in Brooklyn that I didn't feel in Milltown. It was edgier, more wild, and thicker. As Dana and I got closer to Paul's, it started getting less populated and more desolate. It was chilly and a little scary, so we held onto each other and walked fast through the darkened industrial area.

Dana and I had been planning this night for the past few weeks like it was the fucking prom. I had to beg someone to trade shifts with me. She had to work until ten. It was pretty late by the time we got out to Brooklyn.

We were buzzed into the two-story building. We made our way up a florescent-lit stairwell and into the open doorway of the spacious loft. The only source of light in the main room came from a giant slide projection on a white wall. We scanned the room, looking for somewhere to settle. Every corner was occupied with clusters of people gripping red solo cups. We landed on the floor under a large window.

A Yo La Tengo album was playing along with the slide show; Dana looked at me and rolled her eyes. Part of our planning ritual was around how we'd be able to make endless fun of the uber hipsterism at a Brooklyn loft party. A young woman dressed in a full black leotard started doing interpretive dance style in the middle of the room. We fell into each other, laughing hard but also trying to keep it contained so we didn't come off as total assholes even though we were acting like total assholes.

"You can take the girl out of Jersey, but you can't take the Jersey out of the girl," I said to Dana.

"Oh my god. *Seriously*," she said.

"Let's find something to drink," I said.

We made our way through the clusters of people, heading toward the kitchen area where we hoped there would be something decent to drink. I was looking forward to seeing Paul, but I also knew that he would be hosting and didn't expect he'd be able to hang with us much. Dana was looking forward to the possibility of making out with someone. We found a couple of open bottles of red wine on the kitchen table and helped ourselves to the coffee mugs from an open shelf. Some people were smoking by an open kitchen window, and we joined them with our mugs of wine. I lit a cigarette for myself and then lit Dana's. When I peered out the window, all that I could see was pure urban industry and grit.

We sat on the sill beside the window cracked open. The three people standing next to us prattled on about an upcoming art and experimental music show at a gallery in the city. Every time someone said something seemingly pretentious, Dana and I looked at each other and smirked.

I finally caught Paul out of the corner of my eye. He was in a small room off the kitchen with a few other people. It looked like he was playing records.

"Yo!" Paul said when he saw us, giving us both friendly hugs.

"What's up with the dancing chick in tights?" Dana asked sarcastically.

"She lives upstairs," he told us, mimicking erratic dance moves.

I sat on Paul's bed, and Dana sat on a desk chair while Paul played jazz records. A few other people sat on the wide plank hardwood floors. Someone rolled a joint and passed it around. I chatted with Paul about people we both knew from college, what we had both been up to since graduation, and where our families lived. Both of our families were originally from Brooklyn or the Bronx but now lived in different parts of Jersey. It was one of those stoner conversations that could have lasted five minutes or two hours. I had fully lost track of time.

I looked toward the other side of the room and saw that Dana was making out with some guy with messy blond hair and a beard. She sat on his lap in the desk chair. Everyone else had left. Paul and I went into the kitchen to get a drink. It was pretty late by this point, and the party was thinning out. One of his housemates and a few party barnacles were still awake, playing weird quiet music in the living room.

We ended up spending the night in the loft. Dana's make out buddy went back to his apartment in Williamsburg, and Paul gave us his bed. He slept next to us on the floor with a nest of blankets. The three of us chatted and laughed until we passed out, a proper sleepover. There was a feeling of comfort that I hadn't experienced in a long time.

In the late morning, Dana and I said goodbye to Paul, crawled over a bunch of sleeping hipsters who were sprawled out on the floor in the main room, and made our way toward the subway. It was cold and clear out. My eyes hurt from the bright sun, and my head hurt from the cheap wine. We stopped off at a bagel shop.

"You like that guy you were kissing?" I asked Dana while we were waiting for our food.

"He's okay. I gave him my number, but who the fuck knows? He works for some fashion magazine. Probably goes out with models."

"Yeah probably," I said, smiling.

"What about Paul? He digs you."

It was Sunday, and couples sat in foggy cafes, reading the paper and probably making epic afternoon plans to go to a museum or a movie. I was broke, slightly hung over, and had to work that night. I didn't know how I felt about Paul. I didn't know if this was the beginning of a friendship or possibly something more. I couldn't tell if I felt a physical attraction, but I did know there was something I liked about him. I knew that it felt good, safe, and familiar to be around him.

"Dude, I don't know. Maybe we're just gonna be good friends," I told Dana.

"Yeah, maybe. But maybe not," she said, laughing.

We sat on a stoop and laughed at the tomfoolery of the previous night while we ate our messy-as-fuck bagels.

Nine

Portland

In the weeks following the terrorist attacks, I took refuge in Drew's house, not wanting to get out of bed in the mornings, not wanting to go out, and not wanting to see anyone. I wasn't afraid of something happening in Portland. I mean, not really. I just couldn't believe that something like could happen anywhere. I couldn't comprehend the scale of those events. I wasn't there when it happened, so it took a while for the reality to fully set in.

Drew would leave for his studio in the late mornings like nothing had changed, because nothing had changed for him. Not really. He was wrapped up in the sensationalism: the media circus and the terrifying imagery. He could see and feel how this tragedy affected people in horrific ways. He even had a work colleague who was almost on the plane that had flown into the Pentagon but had cancelled his flight last minute. But it wasn't as personal for Drew like it was for me. I had a strong relationship with New York; it was where I was from, where I was born, and where my people were from.

I wasn't working like Drew was, so I didn't have that escape hatch. Tim had closed the office the day after the attacks because he had lost a close family friend who worked in the World Trade Center. He immediately went back to Long Island to be with his people. Since I hadn't really settled in after moving my shit into Drew's house, I spent my days in solitude, avoiding the news and rooting through my personal things. It was as if I had gotten lost and was looking for my way back home.

When I lived in the commune house with Mateo, I had desired an escape hatch from my real life. I didn't want to know the person who had fucked things up with Paul. It was as if I was lost for a while and then recently found.

I poured over my photos for hours. They had been stored in shoeboxes that I had stashed in Drew's guest room a few weeks prior. All the snapshots from my old life were lost in time. I saw my family before we moved out to Jersey, back when my parents were still married. We spent Sundays in Brooklyn at my grandmother's house, eating red sauce pasta and falling asleep on the car ride back home to Queens. The innocent pre-adolescent dorkiness. The high school house party photos with the watery beer, the bad hair, and the lost innocence. The college-era beach house rental with the bad seashore-inspired art, the falling apart cedar shingles, and the drunken sunburns.

There were the photos taken at Milltown Tavern on a snowy night when the windows were fogged. I had felt as if I was living in a timeless cocoon of intimate friendships and killer music.

I also came across a batch of photos that gave me a pit in my stomach.

When Paul and I split up, I ended up with our wedding photos. It wasn't something we negotiated. They just happened to end up in a box with my personal things. We hadn't even gotten to the point of putting them into an album. That was something we had planned to do once we got settled in Portland. But settling down never happened. So, they remained in a big stack of paper sleeves. A good friend of mine was the photographer, and it wasn't a formal affair. She basically mailed us the prints along with the negatives and left it to us to get enlargements and an album made.

Paul stood in a black vintage suit. I was in a cream-colored floor length gown. All our friends comingled together at round tables. Our families smiled, happy and proud. It broke my heart because we had broken theirs. We looked so much younger even though it was not even a year and a half prior. It looked as if our whole lives were ahead of us that day because it was. We hadn't even considered moving out west yet.

I sat on the guest futon, weeping for my losses. And for being an asshole because I had thrown so much away.

It had been a little over a year since I had left the east coast. It was time to make a trip. I didn't know when Tim would open the office again. He had emailed and said that it would at least be another few weeks since they were in the process of planning a memorial service for his friend. He wasn't able to pay me for the time off, but Drew let me skip out on rent so I could go back east. I even invited him to come with me.

* * *

We flew into Newark and took the train into Manhattan. I was scared shitless on the plane and was relieved that Drew was with me. There was a super tense vibe in the airport; security overall was intense. By the time we landed, I was emotionally exhausted and couldn't wait to get a coffee and chill the fuck out for a while. We had booked a hotel in Chelsea since Drew could write it off as a business expense. He was going to meet up with a few friends from design school and make it something of a business trip. I considered crashing in the brownstone but didn't want to tell any of my friends that I was coming. I didn't want the pressure to see everyone in case I wouldn't have time.

Since Drew was with me, I wasn't sure whom I wanted him to meet yet. It was such a loaded issue. A year ago, I left married to Paul, and now I was coming back with this other person.

We walked south from Penn Station toward our hotel. It had been about a month since the terrorist attacks, and right away, I noticed a palpable shift in how people were responding to one another. There was a look of empathy amongst strangers that I had never experienced. There had always been this silent understanding amongst New Yorkers to respect each other's personal space, avoid eye contact, and keep the fuck to yourself. And yet, it was also understood that if someone was in need, offer help.

So, in a lot of ways, this tragedy seemed to have broken down a lot of interpersonal barriers. I could feel the shift in the energy.

I also noticed intense, acrid odors that wafted through the air. I was told it wasn't death. It was the building materials, the metals, and the rubber.

We checked into the hotel. It was a strangely cozy place, geared mostly for European travelers. I had never stayed in a New York hotel before, so it was a new experience for me. I felt like a tourist in my own city. I went right down to the corner deli to grab a coffee. It felt good to be in that deli, to hear the deep New York accents, the brusque attitude, the rich smells, and the fast pace that was familiar even though I was a bit out of practice. I appreciated how good it was to have someone make a coffee for me and slam it with a pile of napkins into a paper bag.

When I got back to our room, I sat on the radiator, sipped my coffee, and stared out the window while Drew had a quick nap. I was home, but I also wasn't home.

When he got up, we took showers and left to take a walk. I wanted to stop by the apartment of an old friend of mine from high school. Elise had recently moved in with her wealthy boyfriend around the same time I had moved in with Drew. She had been in the city when the towers fell, and soon afterward, we had talked over the phone. I knew from some of our friends that she was having a hard time processing all of it. I was curious to hear what the experience was like, so I called, and she said it was okay to stop by. She sounded flat and lifeless.

Elise buzzed us in, and we made our way up the elevator.

I had told her that I was coming with a friend from Portland. She knew Paul and I had divorced. She had been at our wedding with her overly controlling boyfriend. While the rest of us were making plans to party after the wedding, she told me that they had to get going. That was the last time we had seen each other.

I hadn't told her that the reason we got a divorce was because I met someone else. I felt she would have judged me. We had become different people and gone in different directions. After high school, Elise went off to college in Maryland, and I stayed behind in Jersey. We remained bonded pretty tight in a way that I was with friends I had known for a long time, but I had always felt shameful around her. Her family was intact and middle class, and they had a cozy house. I had none of those things. Maybe I was drawn to her during this difficult point in her life, because for the first time, she was the one who had the true struggles.

"Who's that guy?" she asked me while Drew was in the bathroom.

"Oh. We used to work together. When I first moved to Portland."

She knew we were together. I could tell that she wanted me to admit it to her. We sat on the couch. She was waiting for me to confess. But I was too distracted by the apartment. It was like nothing I had ever seen before: huge floor to ceiling windows, fancy antique furniture, and high-end kitchen appliances. I knew her boyfriend came from an old money New England family, but I didn't realize what kind of rich. I had never seen that kind of rich before in real life.

"This place is insane," I told her.

"Yeah, it's not too bad…" she said, shyly.

Her mood was somber. I wanted to ask about the day of the attacks but wasn't sure what the best way to broach it would be. Drew came into the living room and said that he realized a friend of his lived only a few blocks away. He wanted to see if his friend was around, so we made plans to meet in Union Square Park in about an hour. Elise got up, and they shook hands. I walked Drew to the elevator, and when I got back to the apartment, a deep exhaustion and a sense of feeling lost came over me.

"You have any tea?" I asked Elise.

"Sure, Ana. You feeling jet-lagged?"

"I guess. I'm just feeling weird about being here. The city feels weird. Like I came back home to an entirely different city."

We took our tea back to the couch. We talked a little about what Elise had gone through over the past month. Her boyfriend had two good friends from college who worked in one of the buildings and never came home after that day. She said people have been walking around like zombies, looking for their loved ones and posting Missing Persons signs. She went back to Jersey to stay with her parents, but after a few weeks, she knew she had to resume her life again. But once she got back to the city, she couldn't get up to go to work in the mornings. She found it impossible to get out of bed. Her boyfriend couldn't understand what was wrong with her. They fought nonstop since she got back. Her doctor wrote up a short-term disability note and prescribed her meds. She was told that she was suffering from post-traumatic stress disorder. She said that everyone deals with traumas in a different way.

"Are they helping? The meds?" I asked.

"Not really. Not yet. It takes a while for them to kick in."

"I'm sorry. I'm sorry you had to deal with this..." I told her.

We sat quietly for a while. I didn't know what else to say. She had always been a stoic person with a good life, and now she was cracked open. The sun was starting to set, and I wanted to get out of there before the American Psycho boyfriend surfaced from work. It had also hit me that my family was so close by. I had planned to hang out in the city for a few days with Drew before going to see them on my own.

"I know you're with that guy," Elise said to me. "He's handsome."

"Oh. Yeah. Well, we're not really together. I mean..."

"I know you, you know. You don't have to pretend. You didn't want to marry Paul."

"What do you mean?" I asked.

"You only did it because you thought it was what you were supposed to do."

I had nothing to add. Her darkness and despair was seeping into me. I suddenly wanted to be back in Portland. I could easily hide there. Nobody knew the person I used to be. I flipped the script, and we talked for a while about some of our old friends. Who had what jobs, who was getting married, and which ones were having babies.

"I wish we could go back to when we were in high school. Getting wasted at basketball games. Not having to give a shit about anything," she said to me.

"I know. Life was different then. Not as intense."

"You look good, though. You seem happy," she told me.

"Thanks," I said even though I didn't believe her.

We hugged in the doorway. We spoke about getting together for dinner later in the week even though I knew it wouldn't happen. Then I ran down the stairs. I didn't want to wait for the elevator.

I headed east on foot toward Union Square to meet up with Drew. It was a glorious fall evening, just enough chill in the air to wake me up. It reminded me of meeting up with friends in Union Square before going to movies, shows, or bookshops. There was that familiar hopefulness that comes with autumn.

In the decades to come as I would return to New York from Portland, this would become my pattern. I would always feel a strong sense of despair when I arrived. It would be as if it took a certain amount of time for my body to physically adjust to being back. And then following the darkness and the despair would be a feeling of tremendous joy.

I sat on a bench in the middle of Union Square Park. There were many people gathered near the subway entrance around a 9/11 memorial. Candles were lit, and there were all these flyers and notes posted for missing people. It had become a place to grieve. It was beautiful and unbelievably sad. I had never felt the heavy grief of others like I had in that moment. I put my head in my hands and wept. I called my brother. He was at work uptown.

"Ma knows you're here with that guy," he told me.

"So..." I said.

"So, she wants to meet him."

"It's not gonna happen," I told him.

"Don't be like this, Ana."

I felt like a kid again. People tried to tell me what to do. I wouldn't have any of it. If I didn't want my family to meet Drew, they wouldn't meet him. These were the times that I felt misunderstood and judged. It was how I had felt my whole life until I moved out to Portland and could hide the fuck away. I was scared enough as it was to be back in Jersey. I had always felt like a total fuck up, and now that feeling was solidified.

In the familiar New York blue evening light, as the sun set over the Hudson River, more people gathered by the memorial. It was getting chilly, so I plucked a scarf from my bag, looped it around my neck, and walked toward the subway entrance. Candles flickered eerily in the near darkness.

My chest was tight with sadness. People stood close; some hugged one another. As I got closer, I noticed Drew standing nearby, taking photos. I watched him from a distance. Here he was in the city that I considered my true home. It was a wild feeling.

I wondered what it would have been like to be here again with Paul. We shared such a strong love for the city. I looked back at Drew and noticed how somber he looked. His long blond hair fell in front of his face. He was handsome like Elise had said earlier.

Something shifted in me. I didn't want to be here with Paul. He was an amazing fucking person, and I loved him, but he wasn't my person anymore. I realized that if I hadn't married Paul, we would have simply broken up like normal ass people, and it would have sucked. But it was the fact that we got married and divorced soon after that made what happened so much more fucked up.

And now the guy taking photos was my person, and maybe it took me moving all the way out to Portland to find him. We had been skirting around each other for months, afraid to get too close because of how we got together.

Because of what other people thought. Because we had both grown up raw. We were scared shit, and I knew that we wouldn't be anymore.

"Hey," I said when I got to where Drew was standing.

"This is intense," he said.

"I know..."

We held each other close and hard. He kissed me on the cheek and pulled me into a sweet hug.

"Hey, you wanna go see a depressing movie at the Angelika?" I asked Drew.

"Uh, yeah. Sure. Okay."

We walked past the grieving people, down University Place, and headed toward Houston. It was like it had always been except the two tall buildings weren't in the sky anymore.

Jersey

Paul and I had plans for lunch in the East Village at one of those all-you-can-eat Indian buffets. I met up with him at the photo studio where he worked, not far from the Flatiron building. I got there a little early and waited on the sidewalk near the entrance. It was a chilly, bustling weekday, and a couple of office workers were taking their smoke breaks nearby, all huddled together in a tight pack near a steam vent. I pictured them going back to their desks afterward and wondered how they would pass their days. I wondered who they would go home to in the evening and what their homes were like.

It reminded me of being a kid and going to work with my mother. She worked as a secretary for a Japanese camera company, and when I went with her to the office on a few occasions, I enjoyed sitting in the break room, watching people pour themselves coffee. I would walk around and check out what people had on their desks: the family portraits, the personal talismans, and the stained mugs. The office workers always looked uncomfortable in their starchy, pressed clothing. The women had on their nylon stockings and heels while the men had their ties hovering over their distended bellies.

I would often think about what it would feel like to take those clothes off at the end of the day when they got home, most likely a great relief.

I started to get cold waiting for Paul, so I walked up the block a bit. A middle-aged man sat in an idling delivery truck. His arm dangled out the window as he held a cigarette. I could hear school kids yelling on a playground somewhere in the distance. I was in a bit of a trance, contemplating the lives of all these Monday to Friday work people when Paul tapped me on the shoulder.

It startled me. I looked up and laughed, and we hugged. He wore black dress pants, a dark blue button-down shirt, and leather shoes. I had only seen him in jeans, T-shirts, and hoodies before.

I felt a little awkward in my ratty Levi's, a waffle thermal shirt, and a vintage swede jacket. None of my friends ever dressed up, especially for work. We were all eternally broke grubs who had to borrow a nice shit if we had to go to a wedding.

I shivered in the early winter cold as we walked across town to the East Village. Paul put his arm around my shoulder. We had kissed on the street the week prior but hadn't seen each other since. So, there was this awkward tension. I enjoyed the kiss good enough and had thought about it for a few days, but then I didn't think about it anymore. I still wasn't sure how I felt about Paul. I looked forward to seeing him again, but I wasn't sure if I actually wanted to kiss him again. There wasn't a yearning.

"Do you like his smell?" Dana had asked me earlier in the week.

"What do you mean?"

"If you like his smell, it means that you like him."

A woman who went by Cat Power was playing at Milltown Tavern that night. We all took turns watching her perform in the back room and couldn't stop talking about the show. Her sweet but emotionally melodic voice touched us in a way that was hard to articulate. It shot into ours guts and made us tear up. We could tell she had a hard time being center stage and that made her more intriguing.

Paul came to see the show that night, and we hung out a bit afterwards. I opened the bar, so I got off early, and we sat together in the café area by the foggy windows. When Pete turned on the overhead lights for last call, I walked Paul outside, and we kissed.

For some strange reason, it was that night after Cat Power played that I ended up telling Mark about getting an abortion. The show must have opened up some old emotional wounds in me. It was super late, and we had all partied a bit at Jerry Russo's apartment. Rob and a couple of other people had scored some coke, so Mark and I left because we didn't want to deal with that tomfoolery. We walked back to the brownstone. He came up to my room to chill a bit since neither of us were ready to crash. We were still hyper from the music, the weed, and the cigarettes. We sat on my futon and listened to Radiohead's album *The Bends.*

I lay down on the floor. The song, "Fake Plastic Trees" was playing. I hadn't said shit to anyone about the abortion other than my brother, and he had stopped asking me about it by that point, figuring the whole thing was over. When we spoke, I said I was fine, so he probably just figured that I put it all behind me. I never did.

The song ended, and I put back on the futon next to Mark, lit another Camel Light, and told him that something happened to me that was heavy.

"I got pregnant over the summer. It might have been Shawn. But I never told him. I haven't told anyone."

"Jesus fucking Christ," Mark said after a few moments, taking a deep breath.

We didn't talk for a while. We just sat there, smoking, looking at the floor, and taking in the music.

"I killed it," I said, laughing.

"What? Fuck. That's intense."

He held me close to his chest. We stayed that way for a while. I always felt the most comfortable with my guy friends ever since I was a little kid and played with the boy across the street in Queens. I had girlfriends, but there wasn't the ease that there was with guys. Mark and I laughed our asses off because I said I killed the baby. We talked about how I didn't want anyone to know, so I took the bus alone to get the abortion. I said that I felt like a sad loser, which made us laugh even more.

He wanted to know if I was seeing that Brooklyn guy now. He meant Paul. I said I didn't know yet. There were too many things going on in my head to even think about what we were to each other.

* * *

Paul and I sat down at an Indian restaurant. When the waiter gave us our heavy white plates, we went up to the buffet. I felt happy for the first time in a while. I liked being in that busy restaurant with all the colors and the smells; it was comforting.

When I was with Paul, it felt like anything could happen and that it would be okay. I could be however I wanted without judgment. We talked about his job at the photo studio, how he was sick of all his annoying clients who were never satisfied, how he didn't have enough time to make his own art anymore because of the long hours, and how life in the city—the crowds, the chaos—was all starting to eat away at his core.

He told me that one of his friends had just moved out to San Francisco. He was thinking of looking for a job on the west coast.

"Didn't you just renovate that loft?" I asked.

"Yeah. Totally. I wouldn't move right away. I could rent it and make some money," he said.

We split the bill and walked toward Union Square. I could tell he was hoping to kiss me. But the farmer's market was going on, and it was super crowded. So, I just hugged him and said that we'd hang out again soon. He said he'd come to Milltown Tavern over the weekend and maybe catch a show. I watched him walk away in those nice clothes.

I bought an apple from one of the vendors and sat on a bench in the middle of the park. I thought about how Paul wanted to move out west. Maybe I'd move out there with him. Fuck everything and everybody. It wouldn't matter if we ended up together or not. If anything, it would be an excuse to live somewhere else for a while. I headed toward the train back to Milltown and felt like I wanted to run down the street.

* * *

Paul and I started hanging out more. I would go to Brooklyn on my nights off to hang out at his loft. We listened to jazz records in his room, made dinner together, and took the subway into the city to check out art galleries and to see films.

One evening, we got out of a movie at the Quad Cinema. I stopped off at the bathroom before we left, and I saw Paul looking at me in a certain way, staring really, as I walked toward him. Nobody had looked at me like that before. It seemed like he was scared of me, and I could tell it was because of how he felt about me. He must've been scared about how he felt. I didn't feel scared with him. I still felt safe, like he would make anything okay.

Even though we didn't talk about it, we were definitely in a relationship. We made out a lot for a few weeks. One night, I said that we should have sex, and we did. It was sweet and kind, and it didn't have an uncomfortable edge to it that I had experienced with previous lovers. Not like with my long-term ex, where sex was used as power. Not like with Shawn where sex was like an addiction. Not like all the miscellaneous lovers where sex was fleeting and empty. Sex with Paul was a new kind of sex for me. I finally wasn't hungry anymore. There were no more cravings.

We talked about moving out to San Francisco or Seattle. We talked about how both of us were born and raised on the east coast but how we wanted to experience different things. We talked about what it would be like to leave our families. Both of them were deep-rooted in these old school cultures. We talked about how nobody left the clans, how people just stayed put and made families out of what they knew and with what they had.

"I'll miss my friends mostly. I could use a break from my family. I'd probably come back after a few years away though," I said to Paul.

"My family is like whatever. I don't think I'd even miss my friends. I just don't feel that close to anybody anymore..."

"Really?" I asked.

"I mean, I have one close friend from high school, but we never really see each other now that I live in Brooklyn. She still lives out in Jersey."

It was a dreary late fall morning. We sat on a big vintage yellow couch in the loft's common area. It was cold, so I sat next to Paul. Both of us huddled under an old afghan. Paul talked about his family. His father died suddenly when he was in high school, and his mom never recovered. He told me that he had a younger brother, and they were definitely close and loved each other, but they didn't have a lot in common. He looked after his brother a lot after their father died, when their mother was incapacitated in her grief. But when Paul left for college, their closeness faded.

"I needed to be by myself," he said.

"What do you mean?"

"I was this normal high school kid with a mom, a dad, and a nice house with a big yard. Then my dad was dead. I went kind of crazy. My friends were scared to be with me like I was going to hurt myself or somebody else. My mother sent me to some dumb shrink who made me play with fucking sand. It was awful." In other words, he left home after high school and decided to also leave the grief behind.

I tried to understand what he was saying, but I had never lost anyone close to me, so I had a hard time relating. But I did remember how my mother was when my grandmother died. She would sit at the kitchen table, smoking and staring into space. She would suddenly scream at me out of nowhere. I was only seven at the time, and I didn't understand that she acted that way because of grief.

Something about what Paul was telling me made me feel uncomfortable. It wouldn't be until many months later that I would realize he had never fully embraced his feelings about losing his father. He never dealt with them. They still lived somewhere deep inside of him.

"Have you ever thought about Portland as an option?" I asked Paul.

"Not really. Why?"

"I dunno. I love that movie *Drugstore Cowboy*. The vibe seems really chill there…"

We got out an atlas and talked about maybe flying to San Francisco, renting a car, and going on a road trip up through Oregon and Washington. We figured we would wait until spring when the weather was better. I would have to hustle like crazy to save enough money. I'd have to pick up as many bar shifts as possible. I'd have to work more with Rob during the day too, which was something I started slacking off on since I was in Brooklyn more.

We hatched a plan that morning in the freezing loft. We'd save for the next few months, so we could afford to take a trip out west. We even talked about what it would cost to move. Paul made a decent salary at the photo studio, but his rent was high, and he was still paying off the debt from renovating the loft. My rent was cheap, but I still lived shift to shift. I had never been good at saving. If I had money, and no bills were due, I bought shit or went out to eat. I would need to pull it together.

"What if I moved into the loft? Just for a few months, so we could both save..." I said.

"What? And commute to Milltown?"

"I guess. I dunno. I'm just thinking of options..."

It was Sunday, and I had to work that night. Paul said we'd talk about things the following week. He told me that he wanted to work on his art projects, which was something I didn't fully understand and made me feel a little sad. Like he'd rather work on art instead of hanging out with me.

I walked down Bedford to the subway, and on the way back to Jersey, I thought about being with Paul and how it felt like such a real adult relationship. I had never experienced it before, and I had wanted so badly. I thought about us maybe living together and moving out west.

When I got to Milltown, I felt a heaviness as I passed the familiar places and people that made me feel secure these past few years. I was sad about the possibility of leaving the place where I had finally become a real person. I thought about Milltown Tavern and how it was more of a home for me than my family ever was .

Maybe I'd just leave for like a year and look at it like I was taking a long trip. I'd seen so many people come and go through Milltown Tavern over the past few years: musicians on tour, artists leaving the country, and random travelers of all kinds. They'd be around, and then they'd be gone. By the time I had forgotten about them, they'd turn up again, talking about their epic adventures. Maybe I'd become one of those people, not just a Jersey girl who never left Jersey.

* * *

We decided to fly out west in early May. When Paul proposed the idea of me moving into the loft, his housemates scowled at the idea of living with a couple. They weren't into it. They thought it would blow their tragic Brooklyn hipster images. So, after New Year's, Paul moved into the brownstone, and he rented his room in the loft. We took the apartment downstairs. Pete and his lady were moving to her aunt's rent-controlled apartment in the city, so we jumped on the opportunity to have our own space.

This was how things were in the brownstone: it always magically worked out. There was a witchy magic to it. I knew if things didn't pan out for me out west, at least I would have a home to return back to.

I didn't tell any of the Milltown Tavern peeps that I was planning on moving, because I didn't want Rob to fire me. He took these things too personally. I told a few people that I was planning a trip out west. I didn't tell my family that Paul moved in with me or that I was maybe moving away. I said we were going to visit some of his friends on the west coast.

I introduced Paul to my family on Christmas Eve. It was the one holiday that everyone on my father's side gets together: all the aunts, the uncles, the cousins, the siblings, and the significant others. I figured it would be easy to get it all done in one foul swoop. Paul fell immediately into the manic, dysfunctional fold. He wasn't intimidated by all the Italian American red sauce insanity, the loudness, the saying whatever the fuck was on our minds, and the lack of personal boundaries.

I met his family over the holidays too. His mother seemed kind of judgmental of me, looking me up and down and not saying much. I figured this was how it was with mothers and their sons. His brother and his girlfriend weren't any better. It was all super awkward. I now had a better understanding as to why Paul left home and never looked back. He didn't seem to fit into that fractured family mold. I never truly felt that I fit into my family either. I had always felt like they didn't fully get me and couldn't accept me for who I was. Even though there were things that I wished were different, I didn't want to come from a different family. They would forever be my people.

A few days after Christmas, my brother and I met up in the city for dinner. We went to a small, classic Italian restaurant in the West Twenties.

"What's up with you and this Paul guy?" my brother asked.

"I dunno. We get along good. We're going on a trip together in a few months."

"I mean, do you think this is a real thing?"

"I think so. Maybe…" I said.

I trailed off from the conversation and rooted around my pasta, while the waiter filled our water glasses. I was flushed with wine and feeling a lot of shame. I had fucked up so many things in my life. I almost didn't graduate from high school because I hated living with my mother, and as the result, I spent way too much time drunk in the woods. I waffled and crawled my way through college and was finally spit out with a useless degree. I was eternally broke in a noncareer job. I had only been with guys who fucked with my head and made me feel crazy.

The thought of my family witnessing me with this functional, kind, and seemingly sane person felt like too much of a risk.

I knew Paul could be seen as a savior to my fucked-upness. My family didn't want to have to worry about me anymore. All they wanted for me was that I was taken care of, because they didn't think I could take care of myself.

"He seems like a great guy, Ana."

"Yeah. He's pretty cool."

"Don't fuck this up," he said, jokingly but maybe not.

We headed onto the freezing cold Manhattan streets and walked a few blocks together to Union Square before parting ways. Soon, it would be the end of the nineties. There was talk of computers crashing and wiping out everyone's bank accounts. The overall vibe was frenetic. But I was more concerned about moving in with Paul. I was more focused on how I would maybe soon be living on another coastline.

I wasn't thinking about something bad. Nothing bad could happen to me now that I was finally getting my shit together. Good things were still to come.

Epilogue

There was a lot of sadness in the months, years really, that it took for you and Drew to love each other. The happiness you could experience, when all of other things in life fell away, was always accompanied by a deep well of grief. So much of this was because of where you had both come from, the families you were born into, and the traumas that came with who you were as people. But this is what brought the both of you together: that strong desire to bring love to the pain.

If you had stayed with Paul—who loved you unconditionally and who could actually see you for who you were—you would never be able to heal. Drew didn't know how to see you then because he didn't know how to see himself. Because of that, it forced you to face all the hard stuff.

It took you a long time to process how much you had hurt Paul. Nothing could dull the sensations of shame, guilt, and despair, even though you tried your best with generous helpings of weed and wine. You knew he didn't want to simply let what happened between the two of you go. He didn't want to let you off too easily. That wouldn't be fair to him.

You stayed in Portland. You stayed with Drew. You often longed for your family and for your old friends.

Sometimes, you would make plans to move back to Jersey, begging Drew to come. He never relented since he was so afraid of a place he knew could eat you up alive and spit you out because sometimes it did. You visited a lot. Sometimes you stayed for months at a time if you could.

The hardest part of leaving and then staying in Oregon for good was being so far away from the people who you loved and who loved you. The eternal missing emotion was the most painful part of trying to make a new home. There would never be the strong bonds of friendship that tied you to your true roots. For a long fucking time, you blamed it on the place. But you knew you couldn't do that. Because it came down to the time in your life and the people from that time and place.

The Salad Days are over, and you're just this person working your way through a day. You do your work, and you think about what you are having for dinner. Maybe you listen to an album or a song that inspires you. Sometimes, you sing at the top of your lungs because you know all the words. Sometimes, the music makes you feel things again, brings you back, and reminds you of someone. You feel those old feelings for those few moments. Maybe you weep. But something about the epic is gone forever. The only reminder being a certain song from a certain show and a certain person standing next to you as you stare up at the stage and sway to the music.

Before you and Paul moved away, you went to see Will Oldham perform as Bonnie "Prince" Billy at Milltown

Tavern. Your last bar shift was the weekend prior; it was the first time you walked into the pub as a patron again. You were just another Jersey girl going to see a band play. It was just like when you were trying to make something of yourself, figuring out who the hell you were. It was when you were still chasing the dream of getting the fuck out of the stifling Jersey suburbs.

Will Oldham covered The Cranberries song, "Dreaming My Dreams" that night. For years to come, you would remember that song and think about that night. When you rocked forward and back slowly next to Paul. It was one of those moments you don't want to end. You knew you have all these things ahead of you, but it was just so safe and secure in that space and part of you didn't want to leave. But then the song ended, and the band finished the set. You left the pub and your friends for a whole new coastline. You left and never returned as the same person again.

Before you left though, you stood side by side with Rob against the wall by the jukebox. You didn't face each other when you spoke. You looked out over at the bar, the crowd, or the tables like you always had.

"Thank you," you said.

"You'll be back," he told you and kissed you on the cheek.

Years later, when you found out that Milltown Tavern was closing its doors for good, it felt like someone had died. You sat in your backyard, weeding the garden. You were three months pregnant at that point and had been married to Drew for not even a year. Things had been feeling good, hopeful, and stable. You were no longer struggling. Then you got a call with the news.

It felt like the world had closed in around you. You fell to the ground and wept. It was the end of an era, you thought to yourself.

And it was. It really was.

Acknowledgments

Thank you Mike, Butch, Chris R., Chris W., Dana, Eraina, Todd, Mark, Martin, Julio, Louie, Marco, Rody, and all the other ghosts of Maxwell's past. I miss those debauched days.

Thank you Steve Fallon and Todd Abramson for providing me gainful employment and putting up with my twenty-something shenanigans.

Thank you Jenny and Nicol for being both Jersey and Portland. That was a really crazy time for all of us.

Thank you, Jim. I'm sorry shit got so weird. It all worked out well in the end.

And thank you everyone in my life: my family, my friends, and especially my kid. Without you, I wouldn't be able to write this shit.

About the Author

Frances was raised in Queens, New York and Suburban New Jersey, but she now lives in Portland, Oregon with her husband and son. *Salad Days* is her second novel.

About the Press

Unsolicited Press is a small publishing house in Portland, Oregon and is dedicated to producing works of fiction, poetry, and nonfiction from a range of voices, but especially the underserved. Our team has published books that aren't afraid to take on topics of race, gender, identity, feminism, patriarchy, mental health, and more. The team is comprised of hardworking volunteers that are passionate about literature.

Learn more at www.unsolicitedpress.com.

www.ingramcontent.com/pod-product-compliance
Lightning Source LLC
Chambersburg PA
CBHW061613190726
48288CB00007B/2308

9781950730391